Focused on the Father
The Lord's Prayers

Dr. Bob Abramson

Focused on the Father - The Lord's Prayers
Published by Alphabet Resources, Inc.
365 Stonehenge Drive
Phillipsburg, NJ 08865
1-561-963-0778
Dr.Bob@mentoringministry.com

Cover design by Ryan Stacey

ISBN 978-0-9846580-1-5

Contact Dr. Abramson by visiting
www.mentoringministry.com

Reflections on The Lord's Prayer

Edward McKendree Bounds

""As He (Jesus) was praying," so are we to be praying... Certainly if we are his, if we love him, if we live for him and if we live close to him, we will catch the contagion of his praying life, both on earth and in heaven."

"How these simple elements of prayer as given by our Lord commend themselves to us! This prayer is for us as well as for those to whom it was first given. It is for the child in the A B C of prayer, and it is for the graduate of the highest institutions of learning. It is a personal prayer, reaching to all our needs and covering all our sins. It is the highest form of prayer for others. As the scholar can never in all his after studies or learning dispense with his A B C, and as the alphabet gives form, color, and expression to all after learning, impregnating all, and grounding all, so the learner in Christ can never dispense with the Lord's Prayer. But he may make it form the basis of his higher praying..."

(From "The Complete Works of E. M. Bounds on Prayer[1]")

---

[1] Compilation copyright © 1990 by Baker Book House, Grand Rapids Michigan. Quotes are taken from Pages 256 and 268.

i.

Table of Contents

Four
More Prayers: Son to Father

Five
The End was Only the Beginning.

Dedication

Dr. Tom Peters, my pastor from the day I gave my life to Christ, has stood by Nancy and me wherever the Lord called us to go. Dr. Peters has been a model of all this book will encourage you and me to be. It is my honor to dedicate this book to him. His example taught me the value of prayer. I know the Lord Jesus Christ is well pleased with him.

Preface
An Invitation to the Reader

I was sitting in the second row in a meeting at my home church, Trinity Church International, in Lake Worth, Florida. The preacher that day was a friend, Bishop Tony Miller. He is a great preacher, leader and most of all, a blessing wherever he goes. At the finish of his ministry that day, he began to walk off the platform. He suddenly stopped. He looked at me, and quite unexpectedly said, *"Bob, the Lord says to write books, not teaching lessons or sermons. Write books!"*

It is now a few years and a number of books later. I have obeyed what the Lord spoke to me through Bishop Miller. I discovered a gift that was hiding in me. It just needed God to release it through a handful of words from a friend. I have enjoyed writing, and have seen and heard evidence that my books have been a blessing. This is not a surprise, because God is in it.

Even as I submitted my most recent books for publication, "Moral Manhood" and "Reflections - A Devotional Journal, Volumes One and Two," I found myself answering my own invitation to a personal pity party. I lamented that I have not sold enough books to satisfy my pride and ego. I heard all those lies that the devil speaks, when he knows someone is obedient and in the will of God. I said to myself, *"I quit! I am done with writing. It is too much effort. Too often, it completely irritates and frustrates me."* Of course, that was not my spirit speaking, but like all of us, I succumbed to the moment. I was done… until, that is, I was undone.

As usual, my undoing was accomplished by the Holy Spirit. He reminded me of what He spoke through Bishop Miller. *"Did I not say, 'Bob, write books?'"* It was not a shout. It was not done publicly. It was that still small voice that cannot be ignored as it penetrates your heart. It was a combination of a rebuke and loving encouragement. The Holy Spirit said to my heart, *"The message is still the same. Write books! Now, what are you going to do?"*

I have found that when God gives me instructions, He will not leave me hanging, or wondering what I should do with them. So, at the moment the Holy Spirit spoke to my heart and reminded me to *"write books,"* He directed me to The Lord's Prayer in Matthew, Chapter 6. The message was clear. If He had spoken it aloud, He would have said, *"Let The Lord's Prayer touch your heart once again. When it finds a home there and it lights up your heart with its depths of revelation, then begin your next book with it."*

God's Word will speak to us if we will listen. Knowing this, I have gone into what you are about to read, filled with anticipation to hear what He has to say. After all, His mercies are new every morning and great is His faithfulness. I am expecting something for both you and me, as I share from my fresh look into Jesus' teaching and prayers. I encourage you to have the same expectation as you read.

God is faithful. Do the same thing the Holy Spirit encouraged me to do. Keep on going in a life of obedience, until you faithfully finish the course of life God has laid out for you… and do it as someone who can say to the Lord, *"I did my best and You did the rest!"*

2 Timothy 4:7 (NLT)

"I have fought a good fight, I have finished the race, and I have remained faithful."

2 Timothy 2:15 (NIV)

"Do your best to present yourself to God as one approved, a workman who does not need to be ashamed and who correctly handles the word of truth."

Handle the pages that follow as both a commentary and devotional journey. You will first encounter The Lord's Prayer in five verses of Matthew. Other Scriptures in which Jesus prayed will follow. Let them all touch your heart and illuminate your understanding. If you will allow them to, they will speak to you. This is because they are straight from Jesus. He sent them with purpose. They have your name written all over them.

Dr. Bob Abramson

4

One

The Lord's Prayer
Giving Glory to the Father

Introduction

The Slopes of the Mountain

For the disciples, and those gathering around Jesus, it must have seemed like any other day in Israel. Perhaps the sun was shining and a warm, gentle breeze was blowing. It would be a good day to go to the slopes of the mountain and sit in the grass. Who could know what the Lord was about to teach those within the sound of His voice? Who could know the countless number of people who would read His words in the centuries to follow? On that day, and continuing on today, Jesus would teach all of us through His great, life-altering words of instruction that we call The Lord's Prayer. Matthew begins his record of this event with these words.

Matthew 5:1-2 (NKJV)

"And seeing the multitudes, He went up on a mountain, and when He was seated His disciples came to Him. Then He opened His mouth and taught them..."

Can you picture Jesus finding an appropriate place where His voice would carry, while those around Him could sit in relative comfort? He gathered His disciples to Himself. Others began to gather around them, each finding a place in the grass. There must have been an expectation in them, knowing that the Master was about to speak. Perhaps the Lord also felt a great anticipation, knowing how penetrating and powerful His words would be.

Jesus knew that His teachings on The Lord's Prayer would open a world of life-changing possibilities for all who would embrace them. As He sat on the slope of the mountain, Jesus began to speak about this unique, revolutionary way of praying. It was to be a lesson, not just on how to pray, but also how to experience the deep foundations of communicating with God. His teaching revealed that prayer would be the basis of Christian character and life. His lesson on that mountain would provide ways that would forever change and guide the hearts of God's children. His instructions revealed how all Christians could voice their petitions in ways that agree with the will of God for His people. In His faithfulness, the Father would respond. Our agreement with God would bring His action. This action would bring change. Jesus set the pattern for the prayer. If it would be prayed and agreed to on earth, it would be honored and agreed to in heaven.

1 John 5:14-15 (NKJV)

"Now this is the confidence that we have in Him, that if we ask anything according to His will, He hears us. {15} And if we know that He hears us,

whatever we ask, we know that we have the petitions that we have asked of Him."

The Spiritual Setting in which to Pray - Matthew 6:5-8 (NKJV)

{Verse 5} "And when you pray, you shall not be like the hypocrites. For they love to pray standing in the synagogues and on the corners of the streets, that they may be seen by men. Assuredly, I say to you, they have their reward."

The Lord began to teach on praying person-to-Person with God. He started by telling them not to be like the religious officials and the practitioners in the synagogues and streets, who often prayed from pride-filled, insincere hearts.

Jesus knew that the heartfelt draw of prayer on God's people largely had been replaced by ritual. In many cases, the appreciation and reverence for God that began with Abraham and Moses was lost. Prayer was no longer a mountaintop experience. Jesus had seen enough of the Pharisees and Sadducees in action to know this. Their hearts were so hardened that they no longer prayed in submission to God, because they no longer knew Him for who He was. Of course, there were exceptions. Many Israelites' prayers were well meaning, but were trapped in the system that had evolved. They now prayed within this system, with its foundations of insensitivity and hardness of heart. E.M. Bounds refers to this, saying, "In the multiplicity of their prayers, they had lost the art of praying."[2] Jesus would speak to this. His teaching would turn many who listened then, and who hear it now, back to God. He began doing so with these words.

{Verse 6} "But you, when you pray, go into your room, and when you have shut your door, pray to your Father who is in the secret place; and your Father who sees in secret will reward you openly."

Verse 6 reintroduced the proper relationship in prayer. This was a life-changing teaching. Jesus taught that personal prayer time was to be an intimate communication and communion with our heavenly Father. Here was a literal example that held deeper figurative meaning that His audience clearly understood. Jesus spoke of going into the prayer closet. Prayer was to be neither a public exhibition of speaking prowess and pride, nor of self-determined, self-justified righteousness. Jesus was not limiting or removing the value of public prayer. He simply spoke figuratively to the condition of our hearts, as we engage the Father in prayer. Even with public prayers, speaking or hearing them among others should not stop them from becoming a personal and private experience. Again, E.M. Bounds wrote, "The teaching of Jesus Christ on the nature and relationship of prayer as recorded in his life is remarkable. He sends men to their closets. Prayer must be a holy exercise, untainted by vanity or pride. It must be in secret... God lives there, is sought there and is found there."[3]

---

[2] The Complete Works of E.M. Bounds on Prayer, © 1990, Baker Books, Grand Rapids, P. 244.
[3] Bounds, P.246

{Verse 7} "And when you pray, do not use vain repetitions as the heathen do. For they think that they will be heard for their many words. {8} Therefore do not be like them. For your Father knows the things you have need of before you ask Him..."

In Verse 7, Jesus clearly warns not to look for value in empty prayers of repetition, or purely liturgical, religious forms of prayer. He reminds us that God listens to the heart. We could say that our heavenly Father reads between the lines to find the deeper meanings that the words themselves hold. He does not respond to how they sound or whether they resonate with apparent holiness. It is the treasure of a person's heart, exposed in his or her words, that moves Him. The Lord's instruction was simple to understand, yet filled to overflowing with heavenly wisdom.

Pray from the Heart.

Luke 6:45 (NKJV)

"A good man out of the good treasure of his heart brings forth good; and an evil man out of the evil treasure of his heart brings forth evil. For out of the abundance of the heart his mouth speaks."

The Lord's Prayer is to be prayed, or used as a pattern for prayer, from deep within our hearts. The power in the prayer lies within those things to which our hearts have given an abiding and welcoming presence. Here are some critical characteristics that belong in the hearts of those who reach out to our heavenly Father through The Lord's Prayer.

1. Our prayers should reflect the Father's kind of love. As we voice them from within our hearts, they should be intentional, consistent and costly.

The best way I can describe the Father's kind of love is to share with you the definition I came to after years of seeing it at work in my heart and the hearts of others.

> *The Father's kind of love is demonstrated by your intentional, consistent effort to bring as much of His grace, presence and provision to someone, regardless of what it costs.*

Notice the three ways I have described the Father's kind of love. It is (1) intentional, (2) consistent and (3) costly. His kind of love is a pattern to be followed. It is to be demonstrated and delivered straight from the heart, regardless of what it costs. This is *"agape"* or God's kind of love. Anything else falls short of the definition.

Kenneth Hagin wrote this about love. "This *agape* love - this God-kind of love - involves a choice of your will… That love is inside your spirit if you are born again. But you are the one who has to will to put it into practice. You choose to let that love loose from within you."[4]

"Agape" love is not just a concept. As you immerse yourself in The Lord's Prayer, *"agape"* love becomes the spiritual place in which you erect your altar of communion, petition and praise. Do not miss the

---

[4] Hagin, Kenneth E., The Art of Prayer, © 1992 Rhema Bible Church, AKA Kenneth Hagin Ministries, Inc., P.46.

opportunity to come to this altar as often as you can. It is your meeting place with the Father. There you will give everything and He will give back to you so much more.

2. Have complete trust in the One to whom we ascribe glory and make our petitions. This is vital to your prayers for two reasons. First, the Father responds to belief. Second, your faith gains strength when you voice prayers of trust. In the final analysis, believing is a choice. Be sure you choose to believe by relegating natural circumstances to the place they belong - subservient to the power and will of the Father. Pray with complete trust in Him.

Proverbs 3:5-6 is a particular passage of Scripture with which most of us are familiar. For years, this simple statement of wisdom has reinforced my faith and helped me to press on, always believing that God is faithful. Here is the New Living Translation of it.

Proverbs 3:5-6 (NLT)

"Trust in the LORD with all your heart; do not depend on your own understanding. {6} Seek his will in all you do, and he will direct your paths."

As you pray The Lord's Prayer, use it to elevate your faith. As faith rises, you can confidently ask that the Father's will be done. This is possible because He is completely trustworthy. The beauty of The Lord's Prayer is that it instills a sense of increasing trust every time we pray it. Our words travel from our mouths to our ears. They go down into our hearts, and the change happens. When you pray, you are speaking to an always faithful

13

God. Otherwise, your prayers would be useless hypocrisy. The petitions you ask for are meaningless noise until you acknowledge in your heart that the Father really is trustworthy enough to deliver the answers you seek. Therefore, praying The Lord's Prayer requires that you refuse to depend on your own understanding.

3. Always have reverence for the Father. This is what the Bible calls the fear of the Lord. Always give a place of priority in your heart to the fear of the Lord. It is God's provision for strength and the beginnings of wisdom.

Proverbs 9:10 (NKJV)

"The fear of the LORD is the beginning of wisdom, And the knowledge of the Holy One is understanding."

Reverence keeps you positioned to pray in faith through The Lord's Prayer and any other prayer. To do anything less would be to dishonor God and make your prayers of little effect. Reverence demands you pray to the Father with the imminent expectation that He hears and answers, with your best outcomes in mind.

4. Nourish a desire to listen within yourself as you pray. I have observed in myself and others, that it is easy to pray without hearing our own prayers. It is just as easy to pray, without listening within ourselves for the Father's answer. We cannot normally expect to see the finger of God write His answer on the wall, or cause it to be written on tablets of stone. He most often speaks with a still small voice, as the Holy Spirit communicates to us

within our hearts. Some may call this intuition. I call it the voice of the Lord. When you pray The Lord's Prayer, make a determined effort to allow your prayers to be a two-way communication. As you listen for His voice, you will find it is the Father's good pleasure to speak.

5. Understand that The Lord's Prayer has a primarily devotional flavor. Always sweeten your prayers with that flavor. Doing this sets things right for the condition of your altar.

Though the petitions in The Lord's Prayer have profound meaning, they are not meant to replace your more specific and focused prayers for the needs of the moment. Treat the entire prayer as an opportunity to experience a devotional, meaningful moment with your heavenly Father. Everything else should be secondary to your opportunity to worship and commune with Him.

The Structure of The Lord's Prayer

Matthew 6:9-13 (NKJV)

{9} "In this manner, therefore, pray: Our Father in heaven, Hallowed be Your name.

{10} Your kingdom come. Your will be done on earth as it is in heaven.

{11} Give us this day our daily bread.

{12} And forgive us our debts, As we forgive our debtors.

{13} And do not lead us into temptation, But deliver us from the evil one. For Yours is the kingdom and the power and the glory forever. Amen."

Jesus' instructions were not about praying to Him. He provided a specific model of how we are to pray to our heavenly Father. It is a model without ritual. It lacks the boundaries of religion.

- It is without religious stiffness or formality.

- Its format is built around purity, reverence and love.

- It is free of the Law.

- It is not concerned with structure, but with the issues every believer faces.

- It displays our freedom of access to God, because we are reconciled to Him. We have peace with God and can call Him *"Abba Father."*

Romans 5:1-2 (NKJV)

"Therefore, having been justified by faith, we have peace with God through our Lord Jesus Christ, {2} through whom also we have access by faith into this grace in which we stand, and rejoice in hope of the glory of God."

Prayer between the believer and God is to be modeled no differently than prayer between the Lord Jesus and God the Father. That day on the mountain, the model was given from which we could shape our hearts. Then, our hearts would shape our words and they would be pleasing to the Father.

Matthew 6:9 (ICB)

"So when you pray, you should pray like this..."

The intent of the Lord's teaching was to show us at least two things. First, Jesus shows us the form and pattern of the prayer. (Remember not to make liturgical or religious demands on the form and pattern. Keep it free.) Second, He gives us a simple, comprehensive list of things for which we are to pray.

Divisions of The Lord's Prayer

The Lord's Prayer can be divided into three sections. The first section speaks glory and honor to God. The second is a model for us, as we pray for our needs. These first two sections contain seven distinct sets of communications with God. The third section, which is found in the latter part of Verse 13, is the Doxology. Traditionally, a doxology is a hymn containing words of praise, exalting God. The Doxology of The Lord's Prayer can be divided into four distinct sets of declarations. They speak of (1) His kingdom; (2) ascribe eternal power to Him; and (3) give Him glory. Finally, they (4) speak of submission and agreement with Him, indicating that He is eternally supreme in our lives and in the world. The *"Amen"* biblically denotes agreement and completion with what has been prayed. It further indicates that what has been voiced about the Father is truth. The *"Amen"* tells us that what has been spoken in the prayer is finished. Its words have gone out to God. Now, the words will live until He accomplishes His will by answering them.

The Father, through the Holy Spirit, shapes the world with His answers to prayer. As Jesus sat on the mountain, teaching His disciples, He knew that if they were to shape the world, it would happen through the supernatural intervention of the Father. It would be done through answered prayer. The Holy Spirit would respond, and accomplish the will of God.

On the following page, there is a diagram of the structure of The Lord's Prayer. Look carefully at this diagram. Within its three sections, it leads us into deep places of worship and communion with God. It brings opportunities to plead our petitions. It finishes with additional worship and communion, again giving glory to the Most High.

The Lord's Prayer
Matthew 6:9-13 (NKJV)

Seven Petitions		Four Declarations
I. Giving Glory to God	**II. The Good of His Children**	**III. Doxology**
1. *"Our Father in heaven, Hallowed be Your name.* 2. *Your kingdom come.* 3. *Your will be done on earth as it is in heaven.*	4. *Give us this day our daily bread.* 5. *And forgive us our debts, As we forgive our debtors.* 6. *And do not lead us into temptation,* 7. *But deliver us from the evil one.*	1. *For Yours is the kingdom* 2. *and the power* 3. *and the glory forever.* 4. *Amen."*

ෲ𑀀ෲ 1 ෲ𑀀ෲ

First Petition
Giving Glory to the Father
Our Father's Name

Matthew 6:9 (NKJV)

*"In this manner, therefore, pray: Our Father
in heaven, Hallowed be Your name."*

Below, is the International Children's Bible (ICB) version of
the latter part of Verse 9. Take a moment to meditate on the
fullness of its meaning, and its implications for you.

*Verse 9b (ICB) "...Father in heaven, we pray
that your name will always be kept holy."*

The International Children's Bible illustrates a dimension of
importance to the latter part of this opening verse of The
Lord's Prayer. When Jesus says, *"...we pray that your name
will always be kept holy,"* He presents us with clear
instructions concerning our obligations in prayer (and life
itself). This powerful beginning to the prayer reveals Jesus'
words go far beyond the act of praying. The Lord's intention
was that we would understand that a reverence for God's
holiness is not only to permeate our prayers, but our entire
Christian walk. He makes two points worth emphasizing.

1. The name of the Father is more than an identity tag. It carries value and is something special and spectacular. Notice that Jesus did not say, *"...we pray that <u>You</u> will always be kept holy."* The Father does not need anyone's help to be eternally holy. Holiness is His nature. It is the *"name"* of the Father that Jesus emphasizes. We do not have to look far these days to see how the name of God is spoken so easily in vain.

2. Keeping the name of the Father holy is to be an *"always"* and forever, covenantal responsibility of every child of God.

Your Approach to Prayer

"In this manner"

The best way I know to clarify the Lord's intent behind the words, *"In this manner"* (Verse 9a - NKJV) is to paraphrase them as follows.

> *Here is the approach I want you to take when you begin to pray.*

Jesus began His teaching on The Lord's Prayer with words that spoke of something far beyond a method or formula of religious recitation. He taught the appropriate view of God the Father, and the implications this view held. He took His listeners beyond the context of religion, in which they had been raised. He corrected what they considered the normal way for encountering God. It was time for religion to be replaced by relationship. God's people would belong to a family, whose head is God the Father.

With Verse 9, Jesus began to weave a tapestry of words, showing something far stronger and more beautiful than a pattern for the Jewish sacrificial approach to religion. This sacrificial approach limited their understanding of God to a divine being who was to be feared and who remained unapproachable. Now, He would be their heavenly Father.

Our Father, His Sons and Daughters

"Our Father"

Jesus was the only Person who had the right to redefine our relationship with the Father. Now, prayer would become a visit with a near Relative. In declaring this, Jesus imputed to, or placed upon the disciples the rights and privileges of sons of God. This was revolutionary. It certainly could have caused some who heard this to have a degree of discomfort. Jesus gave them the right to speak directly to God and say, *"Our Father."* This went so radically against Jewish religious thinking of that time that it would stir up persecution, even to the point of Jesus' death and the disciples' martyrdom. There were not then, and never are now, any surprises in heaven. It was all in God's plan.

Biblical Confirmation

The original Greek language in Matthew 6:9 uses the word *"pater."* It simply means a father. It has no divine connotation by itself. However, in the context of The Lord's Prayer, Jesus' use of *"pater"* sent the message that there would now exist a Father/child relationship that was, in many ways, no different from an earthly one. Figuratively speaking, our heavenly Father welcomed his children to climb onto His divine lap at any time and without anyone else's help. We can now approach Him just as a young child would approach an earthly father.

The Apostle Paul's writings confirm the new nature of our relationship with God. The nature of this new relationship validates praying to *"Our Father."* In Paul's epistles, the apostle uses the word *"Abba"* to refer to God the Father. Paul's use of *"Abba"* provides further Scriptural confirmation that we have gained intimate, unfettered access to God the Father. We are adopted into His family through our acceptance of Christ as Lord and Savior. We are sons and daughters of God. As such, we fully enjoy the rights of adoption. This is a legal and theological position that has been settled in heaven. Paul writes the following about this new relationship.

Romans 8:15 (NKJV)

"For you did not receive the spirit of bondage again to fear, but you received the Spirit of adoption by whom we cry out, "Abba, Father.""

Galatians 4:4-7 (NKJV)

"But when the fullness of the time had come, God sent forth His Son, born of a woman, born under the law, {5} to redeem those who were under the law, that we might receive the adoption as sons. {6} and because you are sons, God has sent forth the Spirit of His Son into your hearts, crying out, "Abba, Father!"

{7} Therefore you are no longer a slave but a son, and if a son, then an heir of God through Christ."

Now we can begin to unpack the balance of The Lord's Prayer to help us understand Jesus' intentions concerning our approach to prayer.

His Heavenly Residence

"In heaven"

The Father's residence in heaven is foundational to The Lord's Prayer, and indeed, all Christian prayer. It is the place of His omnipotent, omniscient rulership. It is also the place where divine love abides. When we pray The Lord's Prayer, we know that the One to whom we speak resides there, and from this place, He will exercise His loving grace.

When we direct our prayers to Him, He commands all the resources of heaven. He responds with His creative, matchless word, setting into motion angelic hosts, whom He sends to us as agents of His divine will.

- - - - - - - - - - - - -

Prayer Principle

Our Heavenly Father is always ready to grant us an audience and hear our petitions with interest, affection and grace.

- - - - - - - - - - - - -

Always Keep His Name Holy.
"Hallowed be Your name"

On Page 22, I wrote, "Keeping the name of the Father holy is to be an *"always"* and forever, covenantal responsibility of every child of God." Let us go deeper into this subject. The Father's name represents His nature and character. He is *the* Father. He is completely loving and infallible. He makes no error in His fatherhood. We can rest in, rely upon and trust Him because of His flawless nature. Within it resides a bottomless well of His complete grace. It provides living waters, which encompass all our provision, protection, and opportunity.

Seven hundred years before Jesus taught The Lord's Prayer, the Prophet Isaiah was given a vision of the throne of God. He saw its brilliant glory. He proclaimed the Father as King. Isaiah was so struck by what He saw that all he could do was cry, *"Woe is me, for I am undone"* (Isaiah 6:5). Isaiah did this in reverential fear. As we pray The Lord's Prayer, we are to do the same. A.W. Pink, writing about prayer, relates the following quote from W. Perkins.

> "O Lord, open our eyes that we may know Thee aright and may discern Thy power, wisdom, justice, and mercy; and enlarge our hearts that we may sanctify Thee in our affections, by making Thee our fear, love, joy and confidence; and open our lips that we may bless Thee for Thine infinite goodness; yea, O Lord, open our eyes that we may see Thee in all Thy works, and incline our wills with reverence for Thy name

appearing in Thy works, and grant that when we use any one of them, that we may honour Thee in our sober and sanctified use thereof" (W. Perkins)."[5]

It is difficult to get beyond the revelation Perkins had of the name of the Father. His words sound a call to reverential worship before the throne of the Most High.

We ought never to lose that same reverential fear Isaiah had. The beauty of Perkins saying, the "sober and sanctified use" of the Father's name is that we can now approach the King in reverence and so much more. We are joint heirs with Christ, but also sons and daughters who come to the King in friendship and under the covering of His loving favor. How much more should this new standing in Christ motivate us to remind ourselves that the Father is worthy of the highest worship? He has delivered us from darkness into the light of His dear Son Jesus! Let us always hallow His name. Let it always *"be kept holy."* As we set Him above all our personal issues in life, our worship as born-again sons and daughters becomes the legitimate basis for all the requests we make.

Prayer Principle

Keep God's name holy, far above all the personal issues of your life.

---

[5] A.W. Pink, the Beatitudes and The Lord's Prayer, Baker Book House Company, Grand Rapids, © 1979, Published 1982.

Irreverence: Satan's Primary Tool

Think about how much the devil wants you to disrespect your relationship to the Father. If Satan can convince you to lose your fear of the Lord and have a casual, irreverent attitude, he knows it will create distance between you and the Father. An irreverent attitude perfectly describes how carnal desires and self-centered feelings turn us toward exalting ourselves above God. If we accede to this, we buy into the lie that we can elevate our name above the name of the Lord. Satan tried this twice. First, when he was thrown out of heaven with his rebellious angels and then, when he failed to tempt the Lord. Jesus rebuked Him with the Word of God, reminding him of the Father's position over His creation.

Luke 10:18 (NKJV)

"And He said to them, "I saw Satan fall like lightning from heaven.""

Matthew 4:8-10 (NKJV)

"Again, the devil took Him up on an exceedingly high mountain, and showed Him all the kingdoms of the world and their glory. {9} And he said to Him, "All these things I will give You if You will fall down and worship me." {10} Then Jesus said to him, "Away with you, Satan! For it is written, 'You shall worship the LORD your God, and Him only you shall serve.'""

Jesus' refusal to dishonor the Father was evident in the weapons He used to rebuke the devil. It was inherent in the words He spoke. In all Jesus suffered, He never desired any distance to come between Him and His heavenly Father. Knowing that irreverence breeds distance is a warning that can keep us safe. Distance causes a disconnection in any relationship, including, and especially with God. A disconnect with the Father is dangerous. It weakens or kills our ability to communicate with Him. Disconnected prayers are ineffective. Ultimately, they play into the devil's hands because distance diminishes and even cancels the authority we gained as children of the Father. I can imagine that He watches in dismay when this happens, knowing we are playing into the hands of the evil one by positioning ourselves outside the shadow of the His loving protection and provision.

The Solution for Irreverence: Repentance

The beauty of our heavenly Father's character is that even when we treat Him so badly as to disrespect and dishonor Him, He remains available and willing to forgive us. The Parable of the Lost Son (Luke 15:11-32) is perhaps Jesus' best teaching on this truth. In the parable, the father longs for the return of his lost son. The son eventually realizes his error and comes back, seeking nothing except to be near to his father. Then his father forgives and embraces him, dresses him in the best robe and orders a celebration. In this parable, Jesus presents us with a picture of the power of repentance, wrapped in the emotions of our loving heavenly Father.

Luke 15:21-23 (NKJV)

"And the son said to him, 'Father, I have sinned against heaven and in your sight, and am no longer worthy to be called your son.' {22} But the father said to his servants, 'Bring out the best robe and put it on him, and put a ring on his hand and sandals on his feet. {23} And bring the fatted calf here and kill it, and let us eat and be merry.'"

- - - - - - - - - - - - - - -

Prayer Principle

When necessary, pray for forgiveness. You will receive it and all heaven will celebrate. Then continue your prayer in the favor of God.

- - - - - - - - - - - - - -

Examine your own prayer life and weigh it against what you read in the principles below.

1. Pray to your heavenly Father from within the context of your privileged, personal relationship as an adopted child of God.

2. Pray with the understanding that your heavenly Father's name is to be hallowed, for He is holy.

3. Pray, expressing your complete confidence that your heavenly Father is able to answer every prayer. Pray this way to build up your faith and encourage yourself.

4. Pray, knowing the death grip of Satan's kingdom has been broken. The mighty and victorious hand of Christ

has set you free. Speak to the Father from within that freedom. Let your words reflect your position in Christ.

5. Do not debate with God or define for yourself what His will is. Simply pray, hear and obey.

As we go through the individual verses of The Lord's Prayer, we will end each chapter with my amplified paraphrase of the verse that we have unpacked. We will also progressively add each to the previous verses. When the study is complete, you will have my entire amplified paraphrase upon which to meditate. This will never compete with or replace the actual inspired words within The Lord's Prayer, but will be helpful for understanding its intent. Here is my amplified paraphrase of Verse 9.

Matthew 6:9

My Amplified Paraphrase

Our incredible and perfect Father of Mercy and Grace, who rules and reigns in majesty in the place of complete and undeniable authority, let Your name be revered and worshiped, as we behold the beauty of Your holiness.

అదితితితి 2 అదితితితి

Second Petition
For the Coming of God's Kingdom
The Divine Purpose

Matthew 6:10 (NKJV)

*"Your kingdom come. Your will be done
on earth as it is in heaven."*

More than a thousand years after Matthew wrote his Gospel, these words were given their own numbered verse. Yet, they cannot be separated from the words of the previous verse. The prayer flows from one to the next, as Jesus speaks of the Father's holiness, His glorious kingdom and divine will. Jesus leaves us no doubt as to the Father's authority. His kingdom and His bidding are to be our paramount priorities. All authority and power rests in the Father. All other authorities, ecclesiastical and secular, are subordinate to Him. They function because He allows them to do so.

The Father has delegated all authority to His Son, the Lord Jesus Christ. Jesus reigns forever as King of kings in the Kingdom of God. The Father crowned Him with this authority in response to His obedience. His kingship was obtained and eternally validated by His death, burial, resurrection and ascension. His incredible act of suffering as

33

the spotless Lamb of God reversed the hopelessness and helplessness inherent in our fallen world. It was the crowning act of sacrificial obedience. It completed the scarlet thread of redemption that winds its way throughout the Hebrew Scriptures, through the Gospels and on to Calvary and beyond. It remains with Christ and His church for eternity.

The Coming of the Kingdom

In the simplicity of Jesus' words, we find three eternally entwined implications for *"Your kingdom come."*

1. Through the gracious will of God, His kingdom began in a manger in Bethlehem. Jesus was born in a stable to a virgin of no import. This does not fit the notion of nobility or plausibility. Jesus was destined to go from these humble beginnings to the glory of being crowned King of kings. This was the eternal will of divinity, accomplished here on earth. It was the opening act of a plan that continues into eternity. It was done in response to the sinful, rebellious condition into which our world had fallen. Jesus, eternally God, had to be born to His human destiny. He veiled His divinity, dressed Himself in humanity and began His thirty-three year journey among men. It would culminate at the cross. It was the will of the Father, fulfilled in obedience by the Son.

2. The second implication of Verse 10 concerns the events that will occur in the end times, when the Lord comes again to obliterate all evil from the earth. This is referred to in the Hebrew Scriptures by the prophets as *"the day*

of the Lord."[6] This refers to the great and final upheaval of Satan's kingdom. Christ's second coming will bring an apocalypse that cannot fully be described with John the Revelator's words in the Book of Revelation. It will be complete divine judgment. Death, hell and the grave will be defeated and Satan will be thrown into the Lake of Fire. Nothing will stop the power of the Father's will, as He executes it by His Spirit and through His Son.

Isaiah 2:12 (NKJV)

"For the day of the LORD of hosts shall come upon everything proud and lofty, Upon everything lifted up; And it shall be brought low;"

3. When Jesus said to pray *"Your kingdom come,"* His words implied the inward changes His disciples and those of us who followed could experience. The Father's kingdom would establish itself and reign in our hearts, as we turned to Christ for salvation. Ultimately, following that great *"day of the Lord,"* the new earth and New Jerusalem will become the eternal home of God's people. Then, we can worship and be joyful forever before the throne of God.

- - - - - - - - - - - -

Prayer Principle

God's great desire is that, as we pray, His kingdom establishes itself ever more firmly in our hearts.

- - - - - - - - - - - -

---

[6] At least twenty-six times God's prophets speak of *"the day of the Lord."*

Kingdom Differences

Jesus knew that we would have a daily need to pray for the Father's kingdom to come. At times, our need would even be hourly or minute-by-minute. He knew every day would be filled with challenges for each of us. His instructions for praying *"Your kingdom come"* provided a prayer whose answer would help us navigate through a world largely driven by Satan's will. Below are the defining characteristics of this fallen world.

- Sin fills and corrupts our fallen world. Only with Christ's second coming will things change.

- The current domination of uncertainty, fear, selfishness and evil define the kingdoms of this world. Unrepentant humankind remains at enmity with God. The world cannot find peace. It is subject to its demonic masters until Christ returns for His final victory.

Romans 3:23 (NKJV)

"for all have sinned and fall short of the glory of God,"

James 4:4b (GWT)

"...Don't you know that love for this <evil> world is hatred toward God? Whoever wants to be a friend of this world is an enemy of God."

- The curse of hopelessness, sorrow and regret is upon the unrepentant peoples of our world. They are without power to get beyond the outcomes inherent in the curse.

Galatians 3:10a (NKJV)

*"For as many as are of the works of
the law are under the curse;"*

This world will remain a fallen kingdom until that day when
the Father's kingdom is restored to its fullness. Meanwhile,
our prayers can bring the daily benefits of the Father's
kingdom into our lives now, and as often as we need them.
When we utter this petition, we announce that we do not
have to conform to all that flies in the face of the reign of
God. We are able to overcome these things by Jesus' blood
and our own words of testimony.

Those of us who have called Christ their Lord and Savior are
able to appropriate the Father's authority. We can exercise
dominion over the evil forces that previously ruled our lives.
We can live by faith and declare the power of His blood to
every situation we face.

Revelation 12:11a (NKJV)

*"And they overcame him by the blood of the
Lamb and by the word of their testimony..."*

Galatians 3:11b (NKJV)

"...for "the just shall live by faith.""

Your salvation through Jesus, the only Son of God the
Father, makes it possible for you to be delivered from the
tragic outcomes that accompany living in this fallen world.
There is a new nature offered with the Father's kingdom. As
it comes into the life of a believer, it brings with it three gifts

from God. These are given as replacements for the curse of hopelessness, sorrow and regret that the fallen nature of this sinful life has brought. These three characteristics of the Father's kingdom are: (1) righteousness, (2) peace, and (3) joy in the Holy Spirit. We are taught this in Romans 14:17.

Romans 14:17 (NKJV)

"for the kingdom of God is not eating and drinking, but righteousness and peace and joy in the Holy Spirit."

Romans 14:17 (GWT)

"God's kingdom does not consist of what a person eats or drinks. Rather, God's kingdom consists of God's approval and peace, as well as the joy that the Holy Spirit gives."

As a citizen of your heavenly Father's kingdom, you stand forgiven before Him. He sees you as righteous. You now live in peace with Him. If you allow it to, this gracious gift of peace with God, and the peace of God that goes with it, will make themselves known to you. You have a choice. Will you choose to embrace His peace with a joy-filled heart? Will you choose to allow His kingdom into your life as you distance yourself from the world's kingdom? Arthur Pink wrote the following.

"In praying "Thy Kingdom come," we plead for the power and blessing of the Holy Spirit to attend the preaching of the Word, for the Church to be furnished with God-given and God-equipped officers, for the ordinances to be purely administered, for an increase of spiritual gifts and graces in Christ's members, and for the overthrow of Christ's enemies. Thus we pray that the Kingdom of Grace may be further extended till the whole of God's elect be brought into it. Also by necessary implication, we pray that God will wean us more and more from the perishing things of this world."[7]

Arthur Pink made it perfectly clear that praying *"Thy Kingdom come"* is a prayer for grace to abound in the midst of the sin that so deeply blankets our world. Praying to our heavenly Father for His kingdom to come, within and around us, acknowledges that there is hope through the grace that He gives us. Grace is always able to overwhelm the power of sin. It is always able to bring you peace.

Philippians 4:6-7 (NKJV)

"Be anxious for nothing, but in everything by prayer and supplication, with thanksgiving, let your requests be made known to God; {7} and the peace of God, which surpasses all understanding, will guard your hearts and minds through Christ Jesus."

- - - - - - - - - - - -

Prayer Principle

Prayer is a reflection of the completely sure hope, trust and faith we enjoy as our heavenly Father's children.

- - - - - - - - - - - -

---

[7] Pink, P.96.

 conocno 3 conocno

Third Petition
That the Will of the Father is done
on Earth as in Heaven

Matthew (6:10b - NKJV)

"Your will be done on earth as it is in heaven."

Scripture leaves no doubt concerning the Father's determination that His will becomes your blessing. His will is absolute in its ability and authority to determine the destinies of all who turn to Christ. However, the Father will usually allow you to freely make your own choices. He will respect these choices, even knowing that they can lead you to avoid His will. We often learn from our experiences that our choices were wrong, and then realize His will would have been our blessing. The Father's will is perfect. It always leads to your best interests. In 1884, Charles Spurgeon preached the annual sermon of the Baptist Missionary Society at Exeter Hall. He said this, concerning the will of the Father.

"...the will of the great Father is the sum of all wisdom... He ordains all things according to the counsel of His will, and that counsel never errs."[8]

When you rightly discern the nature of God, you know that praying, *"Your will be done on earth as it is in heaven,"* is to pray that all of God's purposes for your life be fulfilled. As you yield to the Father's purposes, you open the door to them being accomplished in your life. The outcomes of your actions then display and validate your fruitful submission to Him. Do not pass up the opportunity to seek, recognize and fulfill the will of God. Doing this takes you to places where His presence and glory become manifest in your life.

- To pray, *"Your will be done on earth as it is in heaven"* is to pray that the righteousness, peace and joy that Adam and Eve once experienced in God's garden would be your portion. It is a prayer for restoration of the Kingdom of God, just as our first parents originally enjoyed it, prior to their fall into sin.

- To pray, *"Your will be done on earth as it is in heaven"* is to pray that positive changes come to the church. Many of us discuss the will of God more than we walk in obedience to it. This prayer is an encouragement to us to press into a deeper relationship with our heavenly Father. This deeper relationship provides the context in which we, as a church family and individuals, can become His obedient, grateful and fruitful children.

---

[8] Charles Spurgeon, "A Heavenly Pattern for our Earthly Life. A sermon preached on April 30th," 1884, Exeter-Hall - Quote taken from the CD: "Expositor's Bible Commentary, Zondervan.

- To pray, *"Your will be done on earth as it is in heaven"* is to pray that we come to the place where our hunger is for more of Him and less of anything that displeases Him. It is to pray that our affections never be divided.

- To pray, *"Your will be done on earth as it is in heaven"* is to pray that we never hesitate to do the will of God. It is to affirm that God's will is not defined according to anything other than Scripture. We determine to simply hear His loving voice and obey.

- - - - - - - - - - - - - -

Prayer Principle

To pray, *"Your will be done on earth as it is in heaven"* is to agree with, and submit fully to God.

- - - - - - - - - - - - - -

Every Christian is responsible to maintain the standing we have before Him as children of God. We are to keep His will for our futures in our hearts, while stewarding the present in our hands. Invite Him to join you, to use and bless you, as you work to accomplish His will every day. Then, in that day when eternity completely unfolds, you can reap the fullness of the fruit of your decision that His will be done.

2 Peter 3:13 (NKJV)

"Nevertheless we, according to His promise, look for new heavens and a new earth in which righteousness dwells."

The petitions in Matthew 6:9-10 extend upward to God. They teach us how to approach the Father in prayer. The focus of these verses is that our heavenly Father is to be glorified in us in every way. They teach us the proper way to approach God. We are to begin with worship, giving Him glory and acknowledging His will. Then, we can bring to Him our petitions. We are to remind ourselves of the blessing-filled priority of placing His will above ours.

- - - - - - - - - - - - -

Prayer Principle

To pray, *"Your will be done on earth as it is in heaven"* is to fill your heart with the delight and pleasures of blessing God with your worship.

- - - - - - - - - - - - -

Matthew 6:10
My Amplified Paraphrase

Father, let all that makes up Your wisdom and accomplishes Your divine purposes be fully done in this place, in this hour, just as it has always been done in heaven, which is the seat of Your merciful, just and sovereign supremacy.

Let us bundle Verses 9 and 10 together, as we progressively build my amplified paraphrase, chapter by chapter.

Matthew 6:9-10
My Amplified Paraphrase

Our incredible and perfect Father of Mercy and Grace, who rules and reigns in majesty in the place of complete and undeniable authority, let Your name be revered and worshiped, as we behold the beauty of Your holiness. {10} Father, let all that makes up Your wisdom and accomplishes Your divine purposes be fully done in this place, in this hour, just as it has always been done in heaven, which is the seat of Your merciful, just and sovereign supremacy.

Two

The Lord's Prayer: The Good of His Children
(Personal Petitions)

CRSOCRSO 4 CRSOCRSO

Fourth Petition
That we may receive Our Daily Bread

Matthew 6:11 (NKJV)

"Give us this day our daily bread."

As you read the pages that follow, you will see that Jesus arranged the petitions within The Lord's Prayer in a deliberate, purposeful order. The first three petitions, which we have already discussed, are to be prayed to the Father as a means of giving Him glory. His glory is always to be first among our prayer priorities (and indeed, our lives). In this fourth petition, we are taught to pray to our heavenly Father for our needs.

Asking for our *"our daily bread"* is to be our prayer for the routine physical needs that keep us fed and healthy during the day ahead. Now, let us look carefully at Verse 11 and see the intent within the Lord's words.

Two things are readily apparent. First, Jesus intends for us to pray for immediate provision. The term *"this day"* makes unmistakable reference to asking for what we need right now. Expressing this in prayer allows you to focus on today. Second, as you pray *"our daily bread,"* you express confidence that God is your ever-faithful Provider. He will not only provide for you today, but will do so every day. Praying Verse 11 gives you a boost in your faith. As you speak them, the words tie themselves to an abundance of faith that begins to flood your heart.

There is another benefit to praying for *"our daily bread."* Praying for the Father to provide *"our daily bread"* helps us maintain a balanced perspective on those things that would try to tempt us. As you pray to the Father for your daily provision, you are confessing your trust in Him. Doing so keeps your flesh in check. It does this by denouncing and rejecting any attraction to greed, covetousness or dependence on someone else to be your provider. Here is a confirming Scripture that makes this principle clear.

Proverbs 30:8 (NIV)

"Keep falsehood and lies far from me;
give me neither poverty nor riches, but
give me only my daily bread."

As you can see, praying Matthew 6:11, puts a strong emphasis on the value of praying for *"daily bread"* as a means of resisting greed and covetousness. You are not asking for luxuries or an accumulation of wealth, just today's provision. In telling us to pray for *"our daily bread,"* Jesus understood that humanity, with its inherent fallen nature, would be easily tempted to try to replace the Father's throne with a throne of self-gratification. The way to overcome this temptation is evident in the restrictive qualities implied in praying for *"daily bread."* We are told to concern our prayers with the moment. Tomorrow will be another opportunity to pray.

- - - - - - - - - - - - - - -

Prayer Principle

Praying today for *"our daily bread"* builds our trust that God will provide for our all our tomorrows.

- - - - - - - - - - - - - - -

God's Obligation

It is God's pleasure to give you your daily bread. In fact, it goes far beyond being just His pleasure to do so. It is His promise and He has made it His personal covenant obligation. He has fully committed Himself to this responsibility. He said in Deuteronomy 28:1-13 that if you would diligently obey His Word, He would obligate Himself to send blessings your way. This includes providing you with your *"daily bread."* He is always faithful to His Word.

Our Responsibility to be Good Stewards

The Father listens for your requests so He can grant them. His expectation is that because you are called to steward all He gives you, that you will take this responsibility of stewardship seriously. Along with the gift of *"daily bread"* comes the accountability for you to utilize it properly, without waste or selfishness. Indeed, the Lord expects you to share what He gives, so that He can provide for others through you. Never view *"daily bread"* as an entitlement. It is always to be seen as a gift of His grace. Be willing to share it because your heart is filled with mercy. Incorporate what He gives you every day to make a difference in the lives of others. God expects you to look upon them with the same heartfelt mercy He has given to you.

- - - - - - - - - - - - - - -

Prayer Principle

As we pray for our "daily bread," our heavenly Father knows exactly what we need. He will not disappoint us. We should not disappoint Him with how we steward what He gives us.

- - - - - - - - - - - - - - -

A Correct Understanding of Daily Bread

All the elements involved in *"our daily bread,"* such as food, clothing and shelter fall under the umbrella of God's faithful desire to care for His children. There is, however, a note of caution concerning our understanding of *"daily bread."* Jesus instructs us that our petitions should address all that is necessary for our sustenance and physical well-being. Our petitions are to be for things we need. There is ample opportunity to petition the Lord for things we desire. He is not opposed to giving them to us. He only requires that they align with His will. Otherwise, they would take us directly to places of covetousness and greed. It is also important to note that physical provision is not the most important thing we need. Jesus repeatedly gives clear instruction concerning the need to live by more than *"our daily bread."* Our emphasis is to be on our eternal bread.

Luke 4:3-4 (NKJV)

"And the devil said to Him, "If You are the Son of God, command this stone to become bread." {4} But Jesus answered him, saying, "It is written, 'Man shall not live by bread alone, but by every word of God.'""

John 6:31-35(NKJV)

""Our fathers ate the manna in the desert; as it is written, 'He gave them bread from heaven to eat.'" {32} Then Jesus said to them, "Most assuredly, I say to you, Moses did not give you the bread from heaven, but My Father gives you the true bread from heaven. {33} For the bread of God is He who comes down from heaven and gives life to the world." {34} Then they said to Him, "Lord, give us this bread always." {35} And Jesus said to them, "I am the bread of life. He who comes to Me shall never hunger, and he who believes in Me shall never thirst.""

John 6:41 (NKJV)

"The Jews then complained about Him, because He said, "I am the bread which came down from heaven.""

(John 6:48 NKJV)

"I am the bread of life."

Christ offers so much more than a day's provision of food or clothing and shelter. He is the Word and the Living Bread! Pray for His grace-filled presence in your life today.

Matthew 6:11
My Amplified Paraphrase

Father, Provide us with those things that will sustain our natural and physical needs through the day and give us Your presence in our lives today!

Let us now add Verse 11 to Matthew 6:9-10, as we continue to build the amplified paraphrase of The Lord's Prayer, chapter by chapter.

Matthew 6:9-11
My Amplified Paraphrase

Our incredible and perfect Father of Mercy and Grace, who rules and reigns in majesty in the place of complete and undeniable authority, let Your name be revered and worshiped, as we behold the beauty of Your holiness. {10} Father, let all that makes up Your wisdom and accomplishes Your divine purposes be fully done in this place, in this hour, just as it has always been done in heaven, which is the seat of Your merciful, just and sovereign supremacy. {11} Father, Provide us with those things that will sustain our natural and physical needs through the day and give us Your presence in our lives today!

ॐౠౚౝ 5 ౠౚౝ

Fifth Petition
That we may be Forgiven and live in Forgiveness toward Others

Matthew 6:12 (NKJV)

"And forgive us our debts, As we forgive our debtors."

Many years ago, I heard a story about two sisters, originally told by Robert Lewis Stevenson in 1903. It is a worthy beginning to this chapter.

TWO SISTERS

A story is told of two unmarried sisters who were life-long church-going women who lived together their entire lives. One became offended by something her sister had said. In fact, she was so offended that she stopped speaking to her sister. The other sister, not to be outdone, did the same. There they lived, each with feelings of anger, bitterness and unforgiveness toward the other. There was no reconciling them.

They continued to live together in their small home. They slept in the same bedroom they had always shared. They painted a line, dividing the sleeping area into two halves from the doorway to the other end of the bedroom. Each of them could come and go without trespassing on the other's side of the room.

In the black of night, each could hear the breathing of the other. For years, they coexisted in silence. Neither was willing to take the first step to reconciliation. Sadly, they never spoke to each other again. Eventually, they died as they had lived, alone and lonely. Even though, through all those years, they lived close enough to hear each other breathing in the night, they never had the comfort of each other's presence.[9]

Jesus' teachings throughout the Gospels inform us that our heavenly Father does not separate receiving His forgiveness from giving our forgiveness to others. They operate together as part of a divinely intended flow in the believer's life. In The Lord's Prayer, Jesus instructs us that this principle of forgiveness is to be verbalized in communion with the Father. This is to be the Christian way of life.

The Petition for Forgiveness
(Two Inseparable Parts)

Part One: *"And forgive us our debts..." (NKJV)*

"and forgive us our sins..." (NLT)

Part Two: *"...as we forgive our debtors." (NKJV)*

"...just as we have forgiven those who have sinned against us." (NLT)

---

[9] Robert Lewis Stevenson, Edinburgh, 1903.

God forgives our sins as long as we are willing to forgive others. Though forgiving others may seem impossible at particular times, it is, nevertheless, the divine command. Peter, knowing how difficult it is to forgive, asked Jesus how many times he (Peter) had to try. The Lord's response (below) reveals the answer. A proper interpretation of His answer is that we are to forgive as often as necessary to keep unforgiveness from capturing our lives.

Peter's Question and the Lord's Answer - *"Seventy Times Seven"*

Matthew 18:21-22 (NKJV)

"Then Peter came to Him and said, "Lord, how often shall my brother sin against me, and I forgive him? Up to seven times?" {22} Jesus said to him, "I do not say to you, up to seven times, but up to seventy times seven.""

Jesus' Answer, Illustrated with a Parable

Matthew 18:23-30 (NKJV)

"Therefore the kingdom of heaven is like a certain king who wanted to settle accounts with his servants. {24} And when he had begun to settle accounts, one was brought to him who owed him ten thousand talents. {25} But as he was not able to pay, his master commanded that he be sold, with his wife and children and all that he had, and that payment be made. {26} The servant therefore fell down before him, saying, 'Master, have patience

with me, and I will pay you all.' {27} Then the master of that servant was moved with compassion, released him, and forgave him the debt. {28} But that servant went out and found one of his fellow servants who owed him a hundred denarii; and he laid hands on him and took him by the throat, saying, 'Pay me what you owe!' {29} So his fellow servant fell down at his feet and begged him, saying, 'Have patience with me, and I will pay you all.' {30} And he would not, but went and threw him into prison till he should pay the debt."

Jesus spoke this parable of the kingdom to present a clear, firm warning about the dangers of unforgiveness and the damage it does to us. We are not to treat unforgiveness as an option. It will destroy our relationships, kill our joy and ultimately threaten our salvation. Yes, it will threaten our salvation. The servant in the parable walked in unmerited forgiveness from his master and yet, he had no understanding of its value. He failed to see what receiving forgiveness required of him. The requirement never changes. Jesus instructs us in Matthew, Chapter 5, that if necessary, we are to reorder our priorities and seek forgiveness and reconciliation. Then, we can turn to the Father and pray.

Matthew 5:22-24 (NKJV)

"But I say to you that whoever is angry with his brother without a cause shall be in danger of the judgment. And whoever says to his brother, 'Raca!' shall be in danger of the council. But whoever says, 'You fool!' shall be in danger of

hell fire. {23} Therefore if you bring your gift to the altar, and there remember that your brother has something against you, {24} leave your gift there before the altar, and go your way. First be reconciled to your brother, and then come and offer your gift."

- - - - - - - - - - - - - -

Prayer Principle

Unforgiveness is deadly. If necessary, leave the altar of prayer. Go, ask for forgiveness and forgive. Then, come back and petition your heavenly Father in prayer.

- - - - - - - - - - - - - -

Never allow unforgiveness to dominate you. It will ultimately bring judgment instead of mercy. In addition, between now and the time of God's judgment, unforgiveness will wound you daily. It will be like a thorn in your side. It will rob you of your blessings. You will become its slave. In the end, many of us who gave unforgiveness a home in our hearts will face the surprise of the Lord's rejection - only because of our disobedience to God's command to forgive. Jesus elaborated on this in Mark, Chapter 11.

Mark 11:25-26 (NKJV)

"And whenever you stand praying, if you have anything against anyone, forgive him, that your Father in heaven may also forgive you your trespasses. {26} "But if you do not forgive, neither will your Father in heaven forgive your trespasses."

No Right to Draw the Line

When you became a believer, you forever lost the right to take up an offense and make your bed in unforgiveness. You no longer have the right to *"an eye for an eye."*[10] You have no right to draw the line between your will and the will of God. If you do, you will cloak yourself in darkness. If you wear that cloak long enough, you will wear it into an eternity without Christ. Forgiveness is a powerful, empowering act in which you reject wrong feelings and embrace sound biblical choices. Having done that, you must maintain your forgiveness, even as much as *"seventy times seven,"* or more. This can be difficult, but with God, all things are possible. Is there someone you need to forgive? Now would be an excellent time to do so.

- - - - - - - - - - - - - - -

Prayer Principle

When we disallow the voices of unforgiveness, we allow and empower forgiveness to speak.

- - - - - - - - - - - - - - -

God's kind of love is forgiving, merciful and full of sacrificial grace. We see this in the example of Jesus, who gave us the wonderful patterns we find within The Lord's Prayer. Imagine how it must have been on that day when the young, soon-to-be-apostle John sat on that hillside and listened to Jesus speak of forgiveness. Think about so many years later, near the end of John's life, as he remembered that day in his youth when Jesus taught how to petition the

---

[10] Matthew 5:38

Father. The words of John's First Epistle say it all. Because God so loved us that He sent Jesus… and because Jesus so loved us that He willingly embraced the cross, then we ought to love one another.

1 John 4:9-11 (NKJV)

"In this the love of God was manifested toward us, that God has sent His only begotten Son into the world, that we might live through Him. {10} In this is love, not that we loved God, but that He loved us and sent His Son to be the propitiation for our sins. {11} Beloved, if God so loved us, we also ought to love one another."

You can be well-fed, well-clothed, have a roof over your head and yet, be without hope. Without God's kind of love at work in you, energizing and maintaining a spirit of forgiveness, you face a hopeless end. Pray that you may be forgiven and live in forgiveness toward others. Arthur Pink wrote the following.

"…we are sinners who, out of a sense of God's mercy to us, are disposed to show mercy to others; hence, we are morally qualified for more mercy, seeing that we have not abused the mercy we have already received… We need to pray much for God to remove all bitterness and malice from our hearts against those who wrong us."[11]

---

[11] Pink, P. 116.

Prayer Principle

Forgiveness of sins from God to us, and us toward others, brings right standing with God. It brings favor, blessings and daily grace.

- - - - - - - - - - - - - - -

Matthew 6:12
My Amplified Paraphrase

And cancel the enormous debt we owe You, just as we willingly cancel and forgive every wrong and every debt owed to us by anyone.

As before, we will continue to build the amplified paraphrase of The Lord's Prayer, chapter by chapter.

Matthew 6:9-12
My Amplified Paraphrase

Our incredible and perfect Father of Mercy and Grace, Who rules and reigns in majesty in the place of complete and undeniable authority, let Your name be revered and worshiped, as we behold the beauty of Your holiness. {10} Father, let all that makes up Your wisdom and accomplishes Your divine purposes be fully done in this place, in this hour, just as it has always been done in heaven, which is the seat of Your merciful, just and sovereign supremacy. {11} Father, provide us with those things that will sustain our natural and physical needs through the day and give us Your presence in our lives

today! {12} And cancel the enormous debt we owe
You, just as we willingly cancel and forgive every
wrong and every debt owed to us by anyone.

ෞൽൟ෨ **6** ෞൽൟ෨

Sixth Petition
For Avoidance of Temptation

Matthew 6:13a (NKJV)

"And do not lead us into temptation..."

Temptation

It is never God's desire to tempt us to sin. It is outside His nature to lead us into a place that gives evil an advantage. The idea that God will lead us into temptation flies in the face of His character. Therefore, there must be something more to understand about this petition. It is only when we embrace temptation as an act of our free will, that we enter into this dangerous territory. We make the choice to disregard God's will, His commands, and the leading of His Spirit. This may occur when we feel the stress of adversity. It may also happen when we surrender to the tempting offer of something that appeals to our carnal sensations, such as lust, selfishness, or greed. In Galatians 5:19-21 the Apostle Paul lists a number of carnal invitations to sin. He calls them the *"works of the flesh."*

Galatians 5:19-21 (NKJV)

"Now the works of the flesh are evident, which are: adultery, fornication, uncleanness, lewdness, {20}

idolatry, sorcery, hatred, contentions, jealousies, outbursts of wrath, selfish ambitions, dissensions, heresies, {21} envy, murders, drunkenness, revelries, and the like; of which I tell you beforehand, just as I also told you in time past, that those who practice such things will not inherit the kingdom of God."

Adversity and carnality are consequences of our fallen human condition. God knows that in the midst of any temptation, trial or trouble, we can gain our finest victories. In each victory, we grow in faith, maturity and confidence. This brings us strength to overcome the next challenge and become winners in Christ. As we do, we glorify God and horrify the devil!

We constantly face battles between the desire to do right and our carnal nature with its tendency toward corrupt action. In Matthew 6:13, the Lord instructs us to pray to the Father for help in these battles. In our own strength, we cannot always avoid falling onto these paths of adversity, which lead us toward evil. Praying Verse 13 communicates our desire to the Father to help us be less vulnerable to the traps and snares, that are inherent in our humanity, and repeatedly confront us.

The process of overcoming temptation can work to fulfill God's divine purposes. For example, sanctification (which is the process of becoming more Christ-like) can often best be accomplished in the midst of real difficulties. In these times, we have to reach deeply within ourselves and find the strength to overcome. This provides the Holy Spirit with an opportunity to help us. He becomes the Change-Agent for

66

us. With His help, we grow and emerge far better and stronger for the experience. Our faith and character climb to new, higher levels. We gain a measure of confidence we could not previously have had. All things can work for good, even temptation.

Two Ways to Understand Verse 13a
"And do not lead us into temptation..."

There are two ways to understand Verse 13a.

1. We can look at Verse 13a as a plea not to be exposed to temptation… as a petition for the Father to remove us from facing the battle. In this case, we would be praying, *Father, keep us from ever being exposed to the tough things in life that would challenge us.* This is not possible. None of us will go through a lifetime of experiences without difficult and challenging battles. We all face them.

2. We can understand Verse 13a as a petition to strengthen us when we do enter our battles. In these times, we are praying, *Father, help us not to yield to the temptations, tests and adversities we face. Give us the grace and endurance to gain our victories, and receive the increase.*

- - - - - - - - - - - - - - -

Prayer Principle

When adversities come, heartfelt prayers touch God, and bring us grace, patience and endurance.

- - - - - - - - - - - - - - -

The temptations we encounter always produce something (whether good or evil). As you have seen, God's design for these times is that overcoming temptation requires patience. It also requires faith, as we choose to trust God and His ways, while denying our carnal desires. As we patiently endure in faith, we grow in our abilities to stay above the adversity and come out winners and champions for Jesus. If we fail to trust God, and give in to our carnal desires, the outcome will be dramatically different. James addressed this possibility as he described the process in which we embrace temptation. He wrote that when we embrace temptation, we then find it leads to sin and perhaps even death. The New Living Translation makes this process perfectly clear.

James 1:14-15 (NLT)

"Temptation comes from the lure of our own evil desires. {15} These evil desires lead to evil actions, and evil actions lead to death."

James' words assure us that ascribing responsibility to God for the temptation does not fit the context of Verse 13 of The Lord's Prayer. If we are lured into sin, it is because of our own failure to resist. Having failed, we will now face what could be considerable consequences. Here is how the process works.

1. We dwell on the temptation until we have allowed its attractions to capture us.

2. We give the temptation a home within us.

3. We bring it to life inside and then nurture it until it grows.

4. As it continues to grow, we give the temptation permission to become master within ourselves.

5. Finally, it wreaks sinful havoc in and through us. It inevitably causes destruction and even may bring physical death. As I have said, we, as individual sinners, are wholly responsible for this process.

Temptation Defined

A temptation is an appeal to our carnal nature that presents us with a false promise. It does this for the purpose of denying what God has promised. At its deepest level, the target of the temptation is our faith in God. The purpose of the temptation is the destruction of our character and the denial of our blessings.

Contrast the destruction of accepting temptation's false promises with the opportunities that resisting them bring us. Resistance to temptation provides us with opportunities for proving and strengthening our faith. Resistance gives us the context to build our character into a greater reflection of Christ. When we resist temptation through faith in Christ, four benefits become ours.

1. We are stronger in our resolve to do what is right in God's sight.

2. We draw closer to God and our relationship with Him is strengthened.

3. We become more mature through the experience of resisting the temptation.

4. Our faith increases.

As you can see, overcoming the temptations we face holds within it the possibilities of these results and rewards.

- Increased faith and blessings

- Character that more closely imitates Christ

- Promotion to places where our influence and fruitfulness will more completely glorify God

The Lord's Prayer is a not a prayer of passivity. God expects us to do our part, as He does His. We are to resist our own sinful thoughts and tendencies, as we maintain an awareness of the potentially evil influence of the world's ways upon our thinking. As we do so, we draw nearer to God and His sanctifying influence. Then, we are changed. We become progressively more like Him.

Hebrews 10:22 (NKJV)

"let us draw near with a true heart in full assurance of faith, having our hearts sprinkled from an evil conscience and our bodies washed with pure water."

James 4:8 (NKJV)

"Draw near to God and He will draw near to you. Cleanse your hands, you sinners; and purify your hearts, you double-minded."

Prayer Principle

The battleground is essentially the mind.
Pray to have the mind and heart of Christ.

- - - - - - - - - - - - - -

The Three Temptations of Christ - All Common to Mankind

When Satan tried to tempt Jesus in the wilderness, it was the most significant attempt at temptation that ever has been tried. The Scriptures reveal Jesus encountered three specific temptations. As we look at how He faced and rejected them, we can learn three powerful principles for our own lives. Here is the account from Matthew, Chapter 4.

Matthew 4:1-10 (NLT)

"Then Jesus was led out into the wilderness by the Holy Spirit to be tempted there by the Devil. {2} For forty days and forty nights he ate nothing and became very hungry. {3} Then the Devil came and said to him, "If you are the Son of God, change these stones into loaves of bread." {4} But Jesus told him, "No! The Scriptures say, 'People need more than bread for their life; they must feed on every word of God.'" {5} Then the Devil took him to Jerusalem, to the highest point of the Temple, {6} and said, "If you are the Son of God, jump off! For the Scriptures say, 'He orders his angels to protect you. And they will hold you with their hands to keep you from striking your foot on a

stone.'" {7} Jesus responded, "The Scriptures also say, 'Do not test the Lord your God.'" {8} Next the Devil took him to the peak of a very high mountain and showed him the nations of the world and all their glory. {9} "I will give it all to you," he said, "if you will only kneel down and worship me." {10} "Get out of here, Satan," Jesus told him. "For the Scriptures say, 'You must worship the Lord your God; serve only him.'""

First Temptation: To Turn Stones into Bread

{Verse 3} "If you are the Son of God, change these stones into loaves of bread."

The devil first challenged the Lord by attempting to persuade Him to rely upon His own abilities instead of trusting the Father to provide for all His needs. Jesus' reply to the devil gives us a pattern to follow in every temptation or adversity we face. It is a pattern of trusting the Father for our daily bread, both natural and spiritual. This pattern was declared by Jesus in His first response to the devil.

{Verse } "No! The Scriptures say, 'People need more than bread for their life; they must feed on every word of God.'"

- - - - - - - - - - - - - - -

Prayer Principle

We will need more than bread for our lives. Allow yourself to pray for, and depend completely on the Lord. Feed on every word from God.

- - - - - - - - - - - - - - -

Second Temptation: To Pressure God and Test His Goodness for our Advantage

{Verses 5-6} "Then the Devil took him to Jerusalem, to the highest point of the Temple, {6} and said, "If you are the Son of God, jump off! For the Scriptures say, 'He orders his angels to protect you. And they will hold you with their hands to keep you from striking your foot on a stone.'"

The devil tried to tempt Jesus into testing God. Satan used the Scriptures in a devious and unsuccessful attempt to justify his argument. This is a common trick today. He still tries to get us to justify our actions, in which we pressure or test God to honor His Word. Never think you can "fleece" God. This is an impossibility. It is an affront to His holiness and only serves to weaken your faith. In asking for a fleece, we essentially give our will priority over His. Then, we expect Him to submit His will to ours. Doing this is directly opposed to the first verse of The Lord's Prayer, in which we declare, *"Hallowed by your name."* Jesus' reply to this second temptation was to respond with Scripture. Jesus used the Word of God to declare to the devil that He would trust the Scriptures to validate and guide His determination to be obedient to the Father. We are to do the same.

{Verse 7} "Jesus responded, "The Scriptures also say, 'Do not test the Lord your God.'""

Prayer Principle

Never use your prayers to try to pressure or test the Father to gain some advantage. Respond to pressure by praying Scripture. Prayer defeats pressure.

- - - - - - - - - - - - - -

Third Temptation: To Worship Satan

{Verse 9} "I will give it all to you," he said, "if you will only kneel down and worship me."

This third temptation was offered from the peak of a high mountain. It was the devil's final try to persuade Jesus to worship him as the god of this world. He continues to do this with all of us today. If Satan can persuade you to replace the Father by idolizing something or someone else, he removes you from the divine favor and protection you enjoy. In worshiping anything or anyone other than God, you actually worship the devil. Jesus' reply to Satan and his temptation was simple. He told the devil where to go!

> *{Verse 10} ""Get out of here, Satan," Jesus told him. "For the Scriptures say, 'You must worship the Lord your God; serve only him.'""*

You will face many opportunities to give the things of this world, and thus, the god of this world, a throne in your heart and mind. Jesus' reply again illustrates that every throne in your life is to be the exclusive place of authority that rightly belongs to the God, alone. Ultimately, it comes down to the question of who you will trust, who you will serve, and in whose hands you will place your life. To frame these questions together in one, ask yourself this. To whom will you be faithful, regardless of anything that might try to weaken or destroy your faithfulness?

- - - - - - - - - - - - - - -

Prayer Principle

Every temptation is a great opportunity to pray.

- - - - - - - - - - - - - - -

Studying the three temptations of Christ allows us to affirm the following principles. First, we are to live our lives, trusting in God for everything. Second, we are to feed on His Word daily. Finally, our heavenly Father is worthy of our worship. We must stand firm in our resolve to serve Him without turning to any temptations to worship whatever our flesh or the devil might offer.

Matthew 6:13a
My Amplified Paraphrase

Be the One who faithfully intervenes when temptation tries to intrude on our lives.

Verse 13a, added to my previous amplified paraphrases gives us the following.

Matthew 6:9-13a
My Amplified Paraphrase

Our incredible and perfect Father of Mercy and Grace, who rules and reigns in majesty in the place of complete and undeniable authority, let

75

Your name be revered and worshiped, as we behold the beauty of your holiness. {10} Father, let all that makes up Your wisdom and accomplishes Your divine purposes be fully done in this place, in this hour, just as it has always been done in heaven, which is the seat of Your merciful, just and sovereign supremacy. {11} Father, provide us with those things that will sustain our natural and physical needs through the day and give us Your presence in our lives today!{12} And cancel the enormous debt we owe You, just as we willingly cancel and forgive every wrong and every debt owed to us by anyone. {13a} Be the One who faithfully intervenes when temptation tries to intrude on our lives.

Seventh Petition
For Deliverance from the Evil One

Matthew 6:13b (NKJV)

"But deliver us from the evil one."

(God's Word Translation)

"Instead, rescue us from the evil one."

(King James Version)

"but deliver us from evil"

Deliverance, Rescue and Salvation

As you can see, there are two ways Matthew 6:13b can be interpreted. The first interpretation provides us with a reference to *"the evil one,* who is Satan. It acknowledges that the spiritual battle we fight daily is a personal one against this chief fallen angel of absolute evil. In the New Testament's original Greek language, the word for *"evil one"* or *"evil"* is *"poneros."* Some translations of Matthew 6:13b, including the first two, that I have provided above, record Jesus referring to Satan as this *"poneros" or "evil one."* The body of Jesus' words and those of the disciples clearly shows the devil to be the primary personality driving the hellish forces of evil.

We understand that, in God's sovereignty, He has allowed *"the evil one"* to have his season of freedom. The Genesis Garden narrative readily explains why. It illustrates how evil gained entrance into the world. Satan's continued presence and his liberty to spread his evil is a consequence of that sinful choice made by our first parents.

In The Lord's Prayer, the interpretation of *"poneros"* as a reference to Satan, directs us ask the Father to keep us from the devil's personal intentions toward each of us. We know that Christ destroyed Satan's authority over believers through His victory of the cross. However, Satan retains his power to do great damage to those who do not trust in and submit to the Lord. The evil one's activity since his fall from heaven has not diminished. It seems that it is becoming even more intense as the times proceed toward the end. This is to be expected because Scripture warns us of it. Without God's intervention, we are no match for Satan. With God's intervention, he is no match for us.

The second interpretation of *"poneros"* speaks of the essential character of evil. This interpretation instructs us to pray for help in gaining victory over the constant struggle with our human sinfulness and evil tendencies. Additionally, it petitions the Father to help us resist the evil in the world.

Whether we accept the first or second interpretation of Verse 13b, Satan is not taken out of the equation. He is always there, doing what he can to draw us into any evil with which we might be tempted. The Apostle Paul recognized these sinful tendencies within himself. He wrote about them in the seventh chapter of his Epistle to the Romans.

Romans 7:17-25 (NKJV)

"But now, it is no longer I who do it, but sin that dwells in me. {18} For I know that in me (that is, in my flesh) nothing good dwells; for to will is present with me, but how to perform what is good I do not find. {19} For the good that I will to do, I do not do; but the evil I will not to do, that I practice. {20} Now if I do what I will not to do, it is no longer I who do it, but sin that dwells in me. {21} I find then a law, that evil is present with me, the one who wills to do good. {22} For I delight in the law of God according to the inward man. {23} But I see another law in my members, warring against the law of my mind, and bringing me into captivity to the law of sin which is in my members. {24} O wretched man that I am! Who will deliver me from this body of death? {25} I thank God; through Jesus Christ our Lord! So then, with the mind I myself serve the law of God, but with the flesh the law of sin."

Paul was certain he could not win the battle against his own fallen human nature. He bemoaned this fact and called himself *"wretched."* He was essentially saying that he hated the sin that infected him. He wrote that it would have been an intolerable, miserable state of mind for him without any remedy... except for Jesus. His problem of sin seemed a hopeless situation, but it was not so. It could be turned to victory through Christ. Paul said he would demand of himself that his thinking *"serve the law of God."* Paul continued his thought in these next two verses.

Romans 8:1-2 (NKJV)

"There is therefore now no condemnation to those who are in Christ Jesus, who do not walk according to the flesh, but according to the Spirit. {2} For the law of the Spirit of life in Christ Jesus has made me free from the law of sin and death."

Paul's discourse on the believer's standing with God is a testimony to Jesus' instructions in The Lord's Prayer. Jesus recognized the vulnerability to sin in God's people. After all, He was there when rebellion came to Eden and sin began. The Lord's concern with our ability to get past the sin we face daily is evident in His John 17 prayer to the Father. He offered this prayer on behalf of His disciples, knowing His time of the deep suffering was about to come. He was approaching His destiny at the cross. Even so, His prayer centered on a petition for his disciples to be under the Father's protective wing. His words, just before His arrest, mirrored those recorded in The Lord's Prayer.

John 17:15 (NKJV)

"I do not pray that You should take them out of the world, but that You should keep them from the evil one."[12]

- - - - - - - - - - - - - - -

Prayer Principle

Prayer is to be bathed in unselfishness, regardless of the pressures of the moment.

- - - - - - - - - - - - - - -

---

[12] We will unpack Jesus' prayer in John 17 in a later section of the book.

The Lord knew He could not ask the Father to completely insulate or shelter us from the evil one, or from the essential character of evil (and therefore, sin) with which we struggle. We are to expect the assault to come, but in its midst, we can also expect to recognize it and look to our Deliverer. Referring to deliverance from evil, A.W. Pink, says this.

> ""But Deliver us from evil." This is a prayer, first, for Divine illumination, so that we may be able to detect Satan's devices (II Cor. 2:11)."[13]

Pink gives these additional reasons for praying Matthew 6:13b.[14]

- "For the strength to resist Satan's attacks"

- "To crucify our flesh - to control our evil desires"

- "For repentance when we do succumb."

- "That our souls are restored again to communion with God."

The language of The Lord's Prayer is corporate, not individual. When we pray, we are not to neglect our brothers and sisters in the Lord. We are to pray that all who follow Christ will be granted these same petitions.

- - - - - - - - - - - - - -

Prayer Principle

Expect the assault to come, but also expect the Deliverer to come with the answer to your petition.

- - - - - - - - - - - - - -

---

[13] Arthur Pink, P.126.
[14] Ibid.

With this understanding that the dual nature of evil is both a person and a force, here is my paraphrase this second portion of Matthew 6:13.

Matthew 6:13b
My Amplified Paraphrase

And bring us through the trials and temptations that would test our faithfulness to You and deliver us from the evil one himself ...along with deliverance from the essential character of every evil thing that opposes You, Father.

Verse 13b, added to my previous paraphrases gives us the following.

Matthew 6:9-13b
My Amplified Paraphrase

Our incredible and perfect Father of Mercy and Grace, Who rules and reigns in majesty in the place of complete and undeniable authority, let Your name be revered and worshiped, as we behold the beauty of Your holiness. {10} Father, let all that makes up Your wisdom and accomplishes Your divine purposes be fully done in this place, in this hour, just as it has always been done in heaven, which is the seat of your merciful, just and sovereign supremacy. {11} Father, Provide us with those things that will sustain our natural and physical needs through the day and give us Your presence in our lives today!{12} And cancel the enormous debt we owe

You, just as we willingly cancel and forgive every wrong and every debt owed to us by anyone. {13a} Be the One who faithfully intervenes when temptation tries to intrude on our lives. {13b} And bring us through the trials and temptations that would test our faithfulness to You and deliver us from the evil one himself...along with deliverance from the essential character of every evil thing that opposes You, Father.

Now, let us proceed to the third section of the book, the Doxology. It is a subject of some controversy. This only appears in selected translations.

Three

The Lord's Prayer: The Fitting End - More Glory to the Father

ಚಿಖಿಚಿಖಿ 8 ಚಿಖಿಚಿಖಿ

The Doxology

A Final Acknowledgment of the Father's Supremacy

Matthew 6:13c (NKJV)

"For Yours is the kingdom and the power and the glory forever. Amen."

As you can see, there is no reference to the God's Word Translation, as I had previously provided. This is because there is scholarly controversy over this final portion of The Lord's Prayer.[15] These words do not appear in some translations. For the purposes of our study, and according to this author's opinions, we will proceed with the assumption that the final part of this verse, the Doxology, is part of the original inspired text. We will operate from the belief that,

---

[15] A great many contemporary translations exclude the final words of Matthew 6:13, the Doxology. This exclusion has its origins in what are called, "higher criticisms" of the King James text by two scholars in the Nineteenth Century. Their names were Wescott and Hort. They decided that the majority of later extent copies of the Bible, which did not contain the Doxology, were more accurate than the 1611 King James Version (their opinion, though far from universal). From these men, came the basis for the English Revised Version and subsequently, the majority of contemporary translations. These disregard and do not contain the Doxology. They omit this third portion of Matthew 6:13.

We will not argue this issue of authenticity. As the author of this work, I find myself on the other side of this argument from Wescott and Hort. I accept the Doxology as original to Matthew's Gospel. You, of course, are free to make your own decision concerning this issue.

as with the previous verses, it was delivered from the Holy Spirit's heart, to Matthew's hand. Below is a sampling of translations of Verse 13c that agree with this position.

New King James Version

"For Yours is the kingdom and the power and the glory forever. Amen."

King James Version

"For thine is the kingdom, and the power, and the glory, for ever. Amen."

Complete Jewish Bible

"For kingship, power and glory are yours forever. Amen."

Young's Literal Translation

"Thine is the reign, and the power, and the glory -- to the ages. Amen."

Jesus wraps up The Lord's Prayer by again modeling praise and glory to the Father. He began with it and now finishes with it. Within this ending Doxology, statements of the Father's supreme position over all creation are to be spoken as an appropriate finish to our prayers. The texture of the Doxology's message is to be wrapped in the highest, worshipful adoration and praise. He is worthy! We have the privilege and high honor to declare this truth.

For us to appreciate completely the Doxology, it should be unpacked into these four parts.

1. We can turn our attention to Jesus' affirmation of the Father's dominion over everything. He says, *"for Yours is the kingdom."*

2. We can marvel at how the Lord ascribes the highest degree of power to the Father.

3. We can stand firm in our confidence that all glory goes to the Father forever. His glory is as eternal as He is. Giving the Father glory will accelerate in light of future events. Christ's second coming to this sin-stained earth will bring about the God's sinless, pure, eternal kingdom.

4. Finally, there is the *"Amen."* This is the closing stamp of confirmation and agreement. Jesus teaches us to place it (or comparable declarations) upon our prayers.

- - - - - - - - - - - - - -

Prayer Principle

Make it your habit to finish your prayers by acknowledging the Father in all His eternal greatness.

- - - - - - - - - - - - - -

Now, let us go deeper into these four parts of the prayer's conclusion.

"For Yours is the kingdom..."

We began our prayer with a petition to *"Our Father."* We end it with a declaration that He is our King. He has complete authority over the kingdom in which we live. In the prayer, the term *"kingdom"* refers to both the physical and spiritual aspects of creation. It is a timeless reference.

This dual world (physical and spiritual) is *the* kingdom, not *a* kingdom. It includes all that falls within the Father's sovereign rulership over His creation. The Father has given His authority to His Son Jesus, who is the King of kings. The Holy Spirit shares their glory within the triune Godhead.

Because there is no one higher than our heavenly Father, none can compete with Him for His authority. Throughout time, many have tried, including Satan and his fallen angels. History has revealed, and future history will confirm, that all rebellion against the authority of the King is futile. Its result is eternal damnation. When we recite this Doxology or any of the others in the New Testament, we are declaring our confidence in the Father's complete dominion. He is able to answer and enforce our prayers.

Even though the Father has granted humanity free will, everything that happens or fails to happen does so because He allows it. He holds our destinies in His hands. When we pray, *"Yours is the kingdom,"* we acknowledge this with reverence and thanksgiving.

"For Yours is the kingdom..."
My Amplified Paraphrase

All that ever existed, exists and will exist, both natural and supernatural, is under Your sovereign rule...

"...and the power"

Power is a universally understood principle. Jesus' words in the Doxology form a picture that is as expressively clear as it can be. His words mean the absolute ability and right to act, without any possibility of being hindered or stopped. His right to act is not to be questioned. The Greek word Matthew used for *"power"* in the original manuscript is *"dunamis."* It indicates power that is miraculous or God-sourced. It is power that can suspend and disregard the laws of nature. It can go beyond all human expectations and thinking. Strong's defines *"dunamis"* as *"miraculous power, might, miracle, strength, violence, and mighty (wonderful) work."*[16] This definition is inadequate. There can be no words to describe the entirety of the Father's power. It is without boundaries and cannot be contained.

Jesus teaches that our prayer doxologies to the Father are to center around declarations of His uncontainable power. It is unlimited. It can neither be hindered nor stopped. There is nothing greater. It comes from the absolute greatness of the Father's divine person. Take comfort in the truth that your heavenly Father is able to enforce His will. He is able to care for, defend and provide for you against anything or anyone.

As a believer in the redeeming power of His Son Jesus, you are privileged to be called a child of your heavenly Father. It is your royal heritage. You walk under His divine shadow. You enjoy His promise to be your refuge and fortress. Countless times, I have found occasion to look to Psalm 91

---

[16] Strong's Concordance, through Parson's Technology - QuickVerse 4

91

to remind myself that I am a son of God, and because I set my faith and love upon Him, He will deliver me.

Psalms 91:1-2 (NKJV)

"He who dwells in the secret place of the Most High Shall abide under the shadow of the Almighty. {2} I will say of the LORD, "He is my refuge and my fortress; My God, in Him I will trust..."

The last three verses of Psalm 91 are spoken in a different voice from the previous verses. In Verse 14, the psalmist becomes silent. Now, God begins to speak. Pay close attention to His voice in these three verses. He confirms that He honors you as you place your love upon Him. This is to be your life's greatest commitment.

Psalms 91:14-16 (NKJV) - God is speaking.

"Because he has set his love upon Me, therefore I will deliver him; I will set him on high, because he has known My name. {15} He shall call upon Me, and I will answer him; I will be with him in trouble; I will deliver him and honor him. {16} With long life I will satisfy him, And show him My salvation."

- - - - - - - - - - - - - - -

Prayer Principle

Pray with an awareness of this absolute, unshakeable truth. The Father is there to care for, defend, and provide for you. He is forever faithful.

- - - - - - - - - - - - - - -

All of creation belongs under His power and authority.

Isaiah 40:25-26 (NKJV)

""To whom then will you liken Me, Or to whom shall I be equal?" says the Holy One. {26} Lift up your eyes on high, And see who has created these things, Who brings out their host by number; He calls them all by name, By the greatness of His might And the strength of His power; Not one is missing."

The New Testament epistles give us a number of examples of doxologies that compliment the one in Matthew 6:13. Below is an example that aligns with the declaration in the Doxology that ends The Lord's Prayer. It reaffirms the Lord's instruction to declare the greatness of the Father's power when we pray. In Ephesians 3:20-21, Paul speaks to us from His own amazing experiences with the risen Christ. He declares that the Father's great power covers and watches over us as His children. We are blessed to be able to have God's protection and power, as we use it for His glory.

Ephesians 3:20-21 (NKJV) - A Doxology

"Now to Him who is able to do exceedingly abundantly above all that we ask or think, according to the power that works in us, {21} to Him be glory in the church by Christ Jesus to all generations, forever and ever. Amen"

Prayer Principle

Pray in the confidence of knowing that your heavenly Father has placed in you the potential to exercise the power of heaven to bring your prayers to pass.

"... and the power"
My Amplified Paraphrase

...and the completely dominant strength and ability to enforce your will against all opposition...

"and the glory forever."

The Greek word for *"glory"* is *"doxa."* From it, we get the word *"doxology."* A doxology is an expression of dignity, glory, honor, praise and worship. It is given in submission to the one of whom it speaks. Doxologies at the end of our prayers remind us that what counts is not what we have, but Who it is that has given us all we have. When we speak words of glory and honor, praising God the Father, the Son or the Holy Spirit, we are acknowledging that God is the One worthy of the prayers we have just uttered.

This particular example of a doxology, in Matthew 6:13, makes the logical completion to our petitions. Why would we ask them of someone who lacked the power to grant them? The Doxology essentially sends this message, as we pray it to the Father: He is able to do what we ask. Understanding this is important because it allows our faith to move into action. Equally important is the Doxology's function to remind us that our prayers are never to be instructions to God. They are to be requests for His intervention. He is God. We are not. The Doxology makes this clear. Psalm 8 points to the traditional, timeless use of the kinds of words found in the Doxology, whether speaking or singing to God.

Psalms 8:1, 9 (NKJV)

"O LORD, our Lord, How excellent is Your name in all the earth, Who have set Your glory above the heavens... {9} O LORD, our Lord, How excellent is Your name in all the earth."

Psalm 8 begins and ends with a repetition of the same declaration of praise to God's wonderful name. We can take this same principle (which was apparent in so many of the psalms David wrote, and his contemporaries sang) and apply it to our prayers to the Father. It remains as normative for us as it was for them. That is the point that Jesus was making in His Doxology to His Father.

"... and the glory forever."

My Amplified Paraphrase

We acknowledge that Your incredible majesty, never-ending splendor and divine brilliance are a shining light, without end.

"Amen."

The *"Amen"* in The Lord's Prayer has been timelessly preserved. Yesterday's *"Amen"* is today's *"Amen."* It will remain so tomorrow and into eternity. The original prime root word, from which *"Amen"* was derived, meant, *"to trust, to be permanent, true"* or *"declare as certain."*[17] Nothing could be more appropriate to follow the Doxology than this final declaration of the Father's permanent trustworthiness and truthfulness. When we complete our prayers to the Father with the *"Amen,"* we are confessing that He is forever faithful and true. He can be trusted with our deepest needs and greatest dreams. As John recorded the Lord Jesus' message to the church at Laodicea in the Book of Revelation, he even called Jesus *"the Amen."*

Revelation 3:14 NKJV)

""And to the angel of the church of the Laodiceans write, 'These things says the Amen, the Faithful and True Witness, the Beginning of the creation of God:"

The essence of the Father, Son and Spirit is eternal truthfulness. As we conclude our prayers with an *"Amen,"* we declare this to ourselves and build our faith.

"Amen."
My Amplified Paraphrase

What we have prayed is truthful and we agree with it. We affirm with our voices and believe in our hearts that it shall come to pass.

---

[17] Strong's Concordance, through Parson's Technology - QuickVerse 4

The Lord's Prayer
My Complete Amplified Paraphrase

Our incredible and perfect Father of Mercy and Grace, Who rules and reigns in majesty in the place of complete and undeniable authority, let Your name be revered and worshiped, as we behold the beauty of Your holiness.

{10} Father, let all that makes up Your wisdom and accomplishes Your divine purposes be fully done in this place, in this hour, just as it has always been done in heaven, which is the seat of Your merciful, just and sovereign supremacy.

{11} Father, Provide us with those things that will sustain our natural and physical needs through the day and give us Your presence in our lives today!

{12} And cancel the enormous debt we owe You, just as we willingly cancel and forgive every wrong and every debt owed to us by anyone.

{13a} Be the One who faithfully intervenes when temptation tries to intrude on our lives.{13b} And bring us through the trials and temptations that would test our faithfulness to You and deliver us from the evil one himself ...along with deliverance from the essential character of every evil thing that opposes you, Father. {13c} We acknowledge that Your incredible majesty, never-ending splendor and divine brilliance are a shining light, without end. What we have prayed is truthful and we agree with it. We affirm with our voices and believe in our hearts that it shall come to pass.

Prayer Principle

Begin your prayers by declaring the holiness of the Father. End them by declaring your trust in Him. Then you will say *"Amen" to* His faithfulness.

- - - - - - - - - - - - - - -

Summary of Matthew 6:9-13 Prayer Principles

52. As we pray for our *"daily bread,"* our heavenly Father knows exactly what we need. He will not disappoint us. We should not disappoint Him with how we steward what He gives us.

59. Unforgiveness is deadly. If necessary, leave the altar of prayer. Go, ask for forgiveness and forgive. Then, come back and petition your heavenly Father in prayer.

60. When we disallow the voices of unforgiveness, we allow and empower forgiveness to speak.

62. Forgiveness of sins from God to us, and us toward others, brings right standing with God. It brings favor, blessings and daily grace.

67. When adversities come, heartfelt prayers touch God, and bring us grace, patience and endurance.

71. The battleground is essentially the mind. Pray to have the mind of Christ.

72. We will need more than bread for our lives. Allow yourself to pray for and depend completely on the Lord. Feed on every word from God.

74. Never use your prayers to pressure or test the Father so you can gain some advantage. Respond to pressure by praying Scripture. Prayer defeats pressure.

75. Every temptation is a great opportunity to pray.

80. Prayer is to be bathed in unselfishness, regardless of the pressures of the moment.

81. Expect the assault to come, but also expect the Deliverer to come with the answer to your petition.

89. Make it your habit to finish your prayers by acknowledging the Father in all His eternal greatness.

92. Pray with an awareness of this absolute, unshakeable truth. The Father is there to care for, defend, and provide for you. He is forever faithful.

94. Pray in the confidence of knowing that your heavenly Father has placed in you the potential to exercise the power of heaven to bring your prayers to pass.

98. Begin your prayers by declaring the holiness of the Father. End them by declaring your trust in Him. Then you will say *"Amen" to* His faithfulness.

Four

More Prayers - Son to Father

The Gospels record many occasions on which Jesus spent time praying to His Father. These prayers consistently demonstrate the lessons of The Lord's Prayer. In this section, we will examine some of Jesus' prayers and see what else we can learn from His personal prayer life.

The Ultimate Union - His John 17 Prayer

John 17:1-3 (NKJV)

"Jesus spoke these words, lifted up His eyes to heaven, and said: "Father, the hour has come. Glorify Your Son, that Your Son also may glorify You, {2} as You have given Him authority over all flesh, that He should give eternal life to as many as You have given Him. {3} And this is eternal life, that they may know You, the only true God, and Jesus Christ whom You have sent."

It was a landmark moment in eternity. Jesus was about to offer Himself as the spotless Lamb of God. The quiet intimacy with the Father in which He now prayed could not silence the coming noise of the violence awaiting Him. Jesus now faced the imminence of His coming trials and ultimately His crucifixion. As you consider this, think about the striking parallel between Jesus' opening words in both His John 17 prayer and The Lord's Prayer in Matthew 6. Both prayers begin with a focus on the Father in heaven. Look again at Matthew 6:9, then at John 17:1.

Matthew 6:9 (NKJV)

"In this manner, therefore, pray: Our Father in heaven, Hallowed be Your name."

John 17:1 (NKJV)

"Jesus spoke these words, lifted His eyes to heaven and said: "Father, the hour has come. Glorify Your Son, that Your Son also may glorify You,""

In the earlier part of His ministry, Jesus had begun The Lord's Prayer with instruction to pray to the Father. Now, His hour of trial would soon be upon Jesus. In John 17, He followed the pattern He had given the disciples by beginning His prayer with a heartfelt cry to the Father. He prayed that all He would go through, and whatever glory He might gain from His suffering and sacrifice, would bring glory to the Father *("that Your Son also may glorify You")*. His words showed the completeness and depth of His dedication to the Father. What mattered was that the Father, whose name was to be *"hallowed,"* would be glorified.

Verse 2: His Authority to Give Eternal Life

John 17:2 (NKJV)

"...as You have given Him authority over all flesh, that He should give eternal life to as many as You have given Him."

In Jesus' prototypical fashion, He looked beyond His personal situation and prayed for those whom the Father had given Him. These were His disciples, friends in the immediacy of the coming moment, and all who would faithfully call Him Lord and Savior in the future. I can imagine that the Lord drew strength from knowing the end would be only the beginning.

Christ's words give hope to all of us that we may escape the pain we deserve for our sin. Yet, Jesus had no expectation that He should escape His pain. His obedience to the Father stopped Him from even considering this. Though the path ahead was dark, He knew it would lead to a brighter, victorious day. Verse 2 clearly defines that whosoever accepts the Lord's coming sacrifice, as their way to salvation, would receive their place on what the Bible calls *"the path of the just."* The Father would grant eternal life to as many as He had given Jesus.

Proverbs 4:18 (NKJV)

"But the path of the just is like the shining sun,
That shines ever brighter unto the perfect day."

The Lord's Prayer and His prayer in John 17 both concern eternal life in the Father's kingdom. To live forever with Christ is the perfect will of the Father. What strikes me is that wherever the Bible points to the will of the Father and the establishment of His kingdom, there is never a conflict. Together, they always fit in His eternal plan.

Again: *John 17:2b (NKJV)*

"...that He should give eternal life to as many as You have given Him."

Matthew 6:10a (NKJV)

"Your kingdom come. Your will be done
On earth as it is in heaven."

Verse 3: Picture-Perfect

John 17:3 (NKJV)

"And this is eternal life, that they may know You, the only true God, and Jesus Christ whom You have sent."

The words of Verse 3 are perhaps the best definition I have seen of eternal life. They arguably provide the greatest expression of God's kingdom that can be found in the Bible. They are picture-perfect words, painted with the brush of the infallible Master. Not a stroke is mishandled. The definition is completely focused. It gets to the foundations of eternal joy. Eternal life, or kingdom living, is about the opportunity that all who choose it *"may know You"* (the Father)... *"and Jesus Christ who You have sent (the Son)."* These words draw us joyfully to the great blessing of our salvation, which is our unending relationship with God the Father, God the Son and God the Holy Spirit. Take the time to think about this. Here are just a few of the benefits of this relationship.

- This unending relationship with the triune Godhead brings you a seat in heavenly places with Christ.

- Your salvation provides you a place under the awesome shadow of His Almighty care and concern (Psalm 91).

- The intimacy of your eternal fellowship with the Father enables you to enjoy forever a place at His table.

These are overwhelming blessings. Beyond all of these blessings, an eternity of joy and peace as God's child awaits you. It brings you the opportunity to join with the angels in worshiping the Father, both now and forever. John 17:3 is a full-color verbal rendering of your picture-perfect future in

Christ. It will be a future filled with worship at the throne of God. What could possibly compare?

Verses 4-5: Glory to the Father on Earth

John 17: 4-5 (NKJV)

"I have glorified You on the earth. I have finished the work which You have given Me to do. {5} And now, O Father, glorify Me together with Yourself, with the glory which I had with You before the world was."

In these verses, Jesus' words teach us about the glory-filled unity of the Godhead. Throughout this prayer to the Father, His words never diminish Jesus' divine personhood. It perpetually stands, regardless of what His humanity is about to endure. Christ our Lord was, is, and will always be one with the Father and the Holy Spirit. Though Jesus voluntarily and temporarily veiled His divinity, He never lost it. It always remained intact. It always remained preeminent. Nothing had the power to diminish His divinity. He would accomplish His mission, to finish *"the work which You* (the Father) *have given Me* (the Son) *to do."*

Divine glory is an attribute with no beginning or end. Jesus prayed that His Father would glorify Him in the same manner as the glory Jesus had before He created the world. He displayed that same glory in His crucifixion and death. It wrapped itself in His suffering. When He surrendered His life, the majesty of His glory shook the earth, split the temple curtain and wrought mighty miracles. Graves opened and the dead were raised. As His executioners watched, they could not deny that He was who He said He was.

As Christ suffered the rejection of the Father and died an atoning death for our sins, *you* were on His heart. There are two prominent lessons we can take from this. First, glorifying the Father has a sacrificial, highly personal element to it. Second, it always glorifies the Son.

Verses 6-8: It was a Purposeful Plan.

As we turn to the next three verses of John 17, we can see the continuity they provide the narrative.

John 17: 6-8 (NKJV)

"I have manifested Your name to the men whom You have given Me out of the world. They were Yours, You gave them to Me, and they have kept Your word. {7} Now they have known that all things which You have given Me are from You. {8} For I have given to them the words which You have given Me; and they have received them, and have known surely that I came forth from You; and they have believed that You sent Me."

Verses 6-8 make it clear that the Father purposefully and deliberately had given Jesus His disciples. They were not selected randomly. They were chosen as part of the plan of salvation from heaven. This plan was established in eternity past, before Christ ever came to earth. The disciples were the Father's gift to Jesus, and therefore, His gift to us. Because they received the Father's words through Jesus, they understood that Jesus truly had been sent from the Father. Though they would flee from the terrible trials of Christ, they would later be restored by His resurrected

108

presence and love. Having the Lord's words deposited within them, the disciples spread the Gospel message. They had their part in delivering the hope and truth of the Scriptures to us.

Verses 9-10: Praying for All of Us

John 17: 9-10 (NKJV)

"I pray for them. I do not pray for the world but for those whom You have given Me, for they are Yours. {10} And all Mine are Yours, and Yours are Mine, and I am glorified in them."

Jesus focuses this prayer concerning His disciples upon their coming purpose and the tasks they would have to fulfill. His prayer prophetically announces that all the disciples do, will glorify Him. We can take inspiration and instruction from this. We, as believers in a long line of spiritual descendents of the disciples, are also to glorify Jesus. This should challenge us to measure our own lifestyles and life's work against one primary issue - do they glorify Jesus... and the Father?

Verses 11-13: In the Father's Grasp

John 17: 11-13 (NKJV)

"Now I am no longer in the world, but these are in the world, and I come to You. Holy Father, keep through Your name those whom You have given Me, that they may be one as We are. {12} While I was with them in the world, I kept them in

Your name. Those whom You gave Me I have kept; and none of them is lost except the son of perdition, that the Scripture might be fulfilled. {13} But now I come to You, and these things I speak in the world, that they may have My joy fulfilled in themselves."

Jesus continues by petitioning the Father to keep the disciples firmly within His (the Father's) grasp, and eternally one in spirit with the Godhead. He prays this while still on the earthly side of His crucifixion. Jesus' words ring with confidence that this oneness will allow His joy to be fulfilled in eleven men who had become so dear to Him.

We can only speculate about all that Jesus' joy included, for both the disciples and Him. A significant part of this certainly must have been the joy of knowing His disciples had carried out His purposes after He was gone from them. The beautiful depth of these verses is found in their potential for us. We, like the disciples, may also have His joy fulfilled in us, as we are one with the Godhead and with all those who preceded us into eternity with Christ.

Verses 14-16: Intercession for the Disciples - Kept from the Evil One

John 17:14-16 (NKJV)

"I have given them Your word; and the world has hated them because they are not of the world, just as I am not of the world. {15} I do not pray that You should take them out of the world, but that

*You should keep them from the evil one. {16} They
are not of the world, just as I am not of the world."*

In these three verses, John recorded Jesus interceding before
the Father for the times that would follow His death. Jesus
knew the disciples were about to experience their most
trying personal battles. He knew the extreme pressures and
difficulties that awaited them. Jesus prayed to the Father that
they would be kept from Satan and his evil works. This was
not a prayer to prevent their suffering. All of them would
suffer and many of them would die as martyrs. This was a
prayer that they would be able to fulfill the Father's will and
that nothing would stop them from bringing forth the
Gospel. As I consider this, I cannot help being reminded of
the Lord's earlier prayer in Matthew 6:13. It was always
about the Kingdom of God being established through the
will of the Father. It still is. We too, may face persecution
and ridicule as part of the attack from Satan. Nevertheless,
God's kingdom will prevail.

Matthew 6:13 (NKJV)

*"And do not lead us into temptation, But deliver
us from the evil one. For Yours is the kingdom and
the power and the glory forever. Amen."*

Verses 17-19: Sanctified by the Father's Truth

John 17:17-19 (NKJV)

*"Sanctify them by Your truth. Your word is
truth. {18} As You sent Me into the world, I
also have sent them into the world. {19} And*

for their sakes I sanctify Myself, that they
also may be sanctified by the truth."

Sanctification is the process of bringing our fallen human nature progressively under the influence of our born-again nature. Sanctification is an act of divine grace. We cannot sanctify ourselves, for that would be works, not grace. Our proper response to God's grace in sanctifying us with His Truth is to commit to Christ's Lordship in every area of our lives. Jesus is, after all, our Sanctifier. Only in our submission to Him will we be changed through the application of His Word, and by the power of His Spirit.

Complete sanctification is not possible in this life. However, we can become progressively more like Him and less like the world every day. Here are three ways to understand sanctification. It is…

1. To be progressively separated *from* evil and set apart *to* God.

2. To progressively realize our potential *in* Christ.

3. To progressively enlarge our capacity to bring glory to the Father, through obedience to the *"truth."*

In Verse 19, Jesus prayed, *"I sanctify Myself, that they also may be sanctified by the truth."* He was communicating to the Father His unshakable determination to finish His task of modeling a submissive, godly life. Here, we can again relate this John 17 prayer to The Lord's Prayer in Matthew 6. The kingdom and will of the Father require us to take to heart the truth of His Word. Separating ourselves from evil and setting ourselves apart to God are fundamentally heart issues. They form the foundations from which we can progressively realize our potential in Christ.

Matthew 6:10 (NKJV)

"Your kingdom come. Your will be done on earth as it is in heaven."

Verses 20-26: The Greatness of God's Love - One with the Father, Son and Spirit

John 17:20-23 (NKJV)

"I do not pray for these alone, but also for those who will believe in Me through their word; {21} that they all may be one, as You, Father, are in Me, and I in You; that they also may be one in Us, that the world may believe that You sent Me. {22} And the glory which You gave Me I have given them, that they may be one just as We are one: {23} I in them, and You in Me; that they may be made perfect in one, and that the world may know that You have sent Me, and have loved them as You have loved Me."

These verses touch my heart in a powerful way. I find that they take me to a place where I could fall on my face and cry holy! Think about what it means for us, as unholy, fallen and imperfect created beings, to be invited into a perfection of oneness with the triune Godhead. Amazing grace is the only term I have to describe this. Salvation sets us up for a great many miracles, yet I am sure that nothing could be more amazing than the significance of *"one with Us."*

Some things about the Father and His kingdom can never be adequately explained. Chief among these is what is found in Verse 23, when Jesus prayed, *"I in them, and You in Me; that they may be made perfect in one."* The concept of the Father in Christ, and Christ in us is beyond human understanding. It presents us with the theological dilemma of trying to merge divinity with humanity. This is not a surprise, since this dilemma has been central to the incarnation of Christ. Accepting the idea of the Father being in Christ and Christ being in us can be done only through faith. Any intellectual explanation, no matter how accurately presented, can be void of revelation. It can be lifeless. God is not looking for us to explain this mystery. He desires that we become living demonstrations of it. From the beginning until now, it was never intended to be revealed through an explanation. It was ordained to be demonstrated by the love of God.

John 17:24-26 (NKJV)

"Father, I desire that they also whom You gave Me may be with Me where I am, that they may behold My glory which You have given Me; for You loved Me before the foundation of the world. {25} O righteous Father! The world has not known You, but I have known You; and these have known that You sent Me. {26} And I have declared to them Your name, and will declare it, that the love with which You loved Me may be in them, and I in them."

Jesus' prayer in John 17 declares the tenderness and affection the Lord has for all whom the Father has given to

Him. It leads us to the conclusion that nothing is dearer to Him than those of us who have chosen to follow Him. Jesus ends His John 17 prayer by petitioning the Father for these things. Jesus asked that...

1. all whom the Father had given to Him would be with Him.

2. we would behold His glory.

   This suggests benefits that are yet unknown to us. We will discover and then enjoy these benefits in the presence of Christ and His glory.

3. the name of the Father and the love of God will be woven into our eternal fellowship with the Father, Son and Holy Spirit.

ೞೞೞ 10 ೞೞೞ

The Ultimate Mountain

"Take this cup"

Luke 22:39-46 (NKJV)

"Coming out, He went to the Mount of Olives, as He was accustomed, and His disciples also followed Him. {40} When He came to the place, He said to them, "Pray that you may not enter into temptation." {41} And He was withdrawn from them about a stone's throw, and He knelt down and prayed, {42} saying,

> *"Father, if it is Your will, take this cup away from Me; nevertheless not My will, but Yours, be done."*

{43} Then an angel appeared to Him from heaven, strengthening Him. {44} And being in agony, He prayed more earnestly. Then His sweat became like great drops of blood falling down to the ground. {45} When He rose up from prayer, and had come to His disciples, He found them sleeping from sorrow. {46} Then He said to them, "Why do you sleep? Rise and pray, lest you enter into temptation."

The Mount of Olives was a familiar place to Jesus, although the Bible is silent about what transpired at other times when He would go there. I imagine it must have been a favorite

117

place of communion with His Father. In times of stress, going there would have been a great comfort for Jesus. On this day, it would offer only the certainty of imminent danger. It must have been a moment of unimaginable discomfort. Jesus knew His destiny was upon Him. He knew that He would be arrested, tried, beaten, tortured and ultimately, suffer death by crucifixion. Let us unpack the Scriptures that describe the Lord's time here on the mountain awaiting His arrest.

Luke 22:40 (NKJV)

"When He came to the place, He said to them, "Pray that you may not enter into temptation."

Scriptural parallels can be great teachers. The wonderful thing about the biblical principle of prayer as a remedy to temptation is that it reinforces itself with each repetition in Scripture. Jesus' words in Luke 22 exemplify this. They bring doctrinal confirmation that prayers defeat *"temptation."* Jesus taught this in The Lord's Prayer (Matthew 6:13) and again here in Luke 22. He warned His disciples (and us) to resist the temptations we all will face. James, the half-brother of Jesus, reinforced this in his writings too.

James 4:7-8a (NKJV)

"Therefore submit to God. Resist the devil and he will flee from you. {8} Draw near to God and He will draw near to you..."

Luke 22:41-42 (NKJV)

"And He was withdrawn from them about a stone's throw, and He knelt down and prayed, {42} saying, "Father, if it is Your will, take this cup away from Me; nevertheless not My will, but Yours, be done."

Verse 41 tells us that Jesus withdrew from His companions and knelt alone in prayer. Verse 42 reports that, knowing what was about to occur, He made a request of His Father that He knew could never happen. This was His flesh speaking in the agony of the moment. It was the predictable response anyone would have made. He asked the Father to take away the bitter cup of His coming suffering. However, Jesus knew in His heart that this cup of bitterness and agony was to be part of His destiny. His next words revealed the strength of His devotion to the Father, to the divine plan of salvation... and therefore, to us. He said, *"...nevertheless not My will, but Yours, be done."* This teaches us two things.

1. Jesus loves us so much that He was willing to endure the most horrific experience imaginable for our eternal benefit. God's kind of love knows no boundaries.

2. Though most of us are never likely to experience anything close to the horrors of crucifixion, these words, became the standard for every Christian, in every circumstance: *"not my will, but Yours, be done."* These words again remind us of the parallels between Jesus' various prayers and The Lord's Prayer in Matthew 6:10, when He prayed, *"Your kingdom come. Your will be done On earth as it is in heaven."*

119

A Choice and a Principle

Luke 22:43-44 (NKJV)

"Then an angel appeared to Him from heaven, strengthening Him. {44} And being in agony, He prayed more earnestly. Then His sweat became like great drops of blood falling down to the ground."

Jesus approached His prayer with intense determination. In His worst moment, His choice was to turn to the Father. There, He found strength in the midst of His agony. Again, God used this unimaginable moment, when even the Lord's sweat became blood, to illustrate a choice and a principle. They are found in the words, *"He prayed more earnestly."*

- The choice for us is always whether, in the face of trouble and even desperation, we will turn to God with faith and determination. The option to turn away should be unthinkable. It carries with it no future or blessing.

- The principle is that, though the Father may not remove the bitter cup from us, He will provide heavenly help to strengthen us.

Like so many who have experienced persecution, sickness, loss of loved ones or countless other trials, I have been blessed to embrace the fellowship of the Lord's suffering in the midst of my own painful experiences. The worst of these was the agony of facing the pain and accompanying death-sentence of cancer. I found myself refusing to turn from God to my own pity. I chose to embrace the Father and His promises. He strengthened me in my suffering and brought me through. People may argue with you about many things.

What they can never successfully argue against are your personal experiences. Mine is this. Christ paid in full for my healing. Because of His suffering and death on the cross, He became my strength and deliverance. He is forever faithful and true. He is completely trustworthy and always able. He did it for me. He will do the same for you. Never allow fear or other negative emotions to turn you from having this same testimony. God is faithful. Choose to draw near to Him. He will draw near to you.

Asleep from Sorrow

Luke 22:45 (NKJV)

"When He rose up from prayer, and had come to His disciples, He found them sleeping from sorrow."

The Greek word used in Verse 45 for *"sorrow"* is *"lupe."* It implies sadness, grief and a heaviness that captures a person through his or her expectations of impending disappointment or loss.[18] This heaviness dulls the senses. It saps a person's strength and captures him or her with a lethargic weariness. In verse 40, Jesus had warned His disciples of the temptation to surrender to the sorrow they were feeing. Despite the warning, they fell asleep in its grip. They succumbed to it, just when Jesus most needed their support.

Luke 22:46 (NKJV)

"Then He said to them, "Why do you sleep? Rise and pray, lest you enter into temptation."

---

[18] Strong's Dictionary within QuickVerse for Windows Version 4.0.

When Jesus completed His agonizing moments in prayer, He arose and went to where His disciples were asleep. He awakened them with the admonition to do what He first warned them to do, *"Pray, lest you enter into temptation."* The only way to overcome the *"temptation"* of being captured and imprisoned by the heaviness of their sorrow was to turn to the Father and stay focused in communion with Him. Jesus' prayer in Gethsemane begins and ends with this warning. He utilized it for Himself and encouraged His disciples to do the same. This is a lesson for us. It will help us understand the value of prayer in the face of temptation, heaviness, fear and uncertainty.

The Shadow of His Wings

From Jesus' words, and others written in Scripture, we learn that disciplining ourselves to turn to prayer in the difficult times is a greatly effective way to face every adversity. Resist the devil by drawing near to God and you resist any enticement or natural tendency to accept defeat. Draw near to your heavenly Father in prayer. Doing this becomes the entrance to closeness to Him and the protection you will find under the shadow of His wings. Then, you can face adversity and come away with your heart intact. When you pray, *"Our Father in heaven, Hallowed be Your name"* and ask Him to *"deliver us from the evil one."* (Matthew 6:9 and 13a), you will find your heavenly Father waiting to respond... and He will become your refuge and fortress.

Psalms 17:8 (NKJV)

"Keep me as the apple of Your eye; Hide me under the shadow of Your wings,"

Psalms 36:7 (NKJV)

"How precious is Your lovingkindness, O God! Therefore the children of men put their trust under the shadow of Your wings."

Psalms 57:1 (NKJV)

"Be merciful to me, O God, be merciful to me! For my soul trusts in You; And in the shadow of Your wings I will make my refuge, Until these calamities have passed by."

Psalms 91:1-2 (NKJV)

"He who dwells in the secret place of the Most High Shall abide under the shadow of the Almighty. {2} I will say of the LORD, "He is my refuge and my fortress; My God, in Him I will trust.""

ᏺᏬᏟᏮᏋ 11 ᏺᏬᏟᏮᏋ

His Ultimate Loss - *"My God, My God"*

Mark 15:33-39 (NKJV)

"Now when the sixth hour had come, there was darkness over the whole land until the ninth hour. {34} And at the ninth hour Jesus cried out with a loud voice, saying, "Eloi, Eloi, lama sabachthani?" which is translated...

"My God, My God, why have You forsaken Me?"

{35} Some of those who stood by, when they heard that, said, "Look, He is calling for Elijah!" {36} Then someone ran and filled a sponge full of sour wine, put it on a reed, and offered it to Him to drink, saying, "Let Him alone; let us see if Elijah will come to take Him down." {37} And Jesus cried out with a loud voice, and breathed His last. {38} Then the veil of the temple was torn in two from top to bottom. {39} So when the centurion, who stood opposite Him, saw that He cried out like this and breathed His last, he said, "Truly this Man was the Son of God!""

"Why have You forsaken me?"

You might ask why I would describe the Lord hanging on His cross as His ultimate loss. We know it led to His

125

ultimate victory. (We will look at His victory in a later chapter.) The agonizing words Jesus spoke, as He hung nailed between heaven and earth, were more than cries of physical anguish. They were the mournful expression of the tragic shattering of the divine relationship. Even Jesus could not endure it. This loss was immeasurably worse than His physical suffering. As never before or again, Jesus was completely alone. He had been pulled violently from the foundations and warmth of the triune Godhead and left to hang coldly, alone.

Think of the spiritual position in which Jesus found Himself. Then, think of God's promise to us never to leave us in the position that Jesus was in - separated from the Father and alone. We can easily be tempted to overlook His promise when things turn troublesome and difficult. However, it is a promise based on the Son of Man's ultimate sacrifice in the moments of His ultimate loss. We never will have to experience this same void of cold aloneness that was Jesus' portion in that terrible event.

Hebrews 13:5 (NKJV)

"For He Himself has said, "I will never leave you nor forsake you.""

You can celebrate the promise this verse holds. Centuries before the crucifixion of Christ, David wrote Psalm 27. In it, David spoke prophetically of a promise that would be fulfilled by what Jesus would accomplish in His lonely, agonizing death. It is your promise for today and all of eternity. The Father turned away from Jesus at the cross so that He could promise He would never turn from you.

Psalms 27:10 (NKJV)

"When my father and my mother forsake me, Then the LORD will take care of me."

That Terrible Signal of Wonderful Grace

Mark 15:37-38 (NKJV)

"And Jesus cried out with a loud voice, and breathed His last. {38} Then the veil of the temple was torn in two from top to bottom."

As Jesus breathed His last breath on the cross, the Father must have been unimaginably grieved. His grief would have been so beyond any earthly experience that there is no way we could ever understand how He felt. It was a moment of the deepest darkness. However, it signaled and set in motion three days, following which death, hell and the grave would flee in the face of the newness of the age of grace. The veil of the temple was torn. It was ripped, top to bottom, by a supernatural touch. The past under the Law was now ordained from heaven to be ripped to pieces. It would not be put back in place again. Salvation had come and fulfilled the Law. Salvation provided the way into a relationship in which we would never have to repeat Jesus' words, *"My God, My God, why have you forsaken me?"*

2 Corinthians 5:19 (NKJV)

"that is, that God was in Christ reconciling the world to Himself, not imputing their trespasses to them, and has committed to us the word of reconciliation."

2 Corinthians 5:17 (NKJV)

"Therefore, if anyone is in Christ, he is a new creation; old things have passed away; behold, all things have become new."

Mark 15:39-38 (NKJV)

"So when the centurion, who stood opposite Him, saw that He cried out like this and breathed His last, he said, "Truly this Man was the Son of God!""

Among those who laid their hands to the hammer and nails to kill Jesus, was a centurion who could no longer deny the truth. Truly, Jesus was the Son of God. Can you imagine the awe that moment brought to those who were there? It would have been impossible to deny the supernatural moving of God's hand. It struck a deep cord in the hearts of everyone. Some would repent and others would harden their hearts. Today brings the same reactions. When God moves, some draw near and are brought into His kingdom. Others recoil and refuse His grace.

In the next chapter, we will see how Christ's love expressed His heart of grace at the cross.

His Ultimate Love - *"Father, forgive them"*

Luke 23:33-34 (NKJV)

"And when they had come to the place called Calvary, there they crucified Him, and the criminals, one on the right hand and the other on the left. {34} Then Jesus said, "Father, forgive them, for they do not know what they do." And they divided His garments and cast lots."

In the parallel to Mark 15, Luke 23 reports the Lord's powerful words of forgiveness, just before He died. There is no way to get past this passage of Scripture without being acutely aware of the mind-numbing contrast it presents. Ultimate evil was endured by the purest example of ultimate good. The spotless Lamb of God was slaughtered in complete injustice. There was no mercy, only the harsh execution of an innocent Man. Though the Roman soldiers crucified the Lord without mercy, their actions made the way for us to find mercy. This is the same mercy Jesus had for his killers when He asked His Father to forgive them.

It is fitting that Jesus' companions in that dark hour of death were two condemned criminals. They represented all of humankind, condemned by our sin nature to die. They deserved the punishment they were about to receive. We deserve the same for our sins. However, God's grace says otherwise.

Luke 23:39-43 (NKJV)

"Then one of the criminals who were hanged blasphemed Him, saying, "If You are the Christ, save Yourself and us." {40} But the other, answering, rebuked him, saying, "Do you not even fear God, seeing you are under the same condemnation? {41} And we indeed justly, for we receive the due reward of our deeds; but this Man has done nothing wrong." {42} Then he said to Jesus, "Lord, remember me when You come into Your kingdom." {43} And Jesus said to him, "Assuredly, I say to you, today you will be with Me in Paradise."

"Lord, remember me..."

In that final moment, one of the criminals turned away from Christ, thus sealing his eternal damnation. The other turned to Christ and found his eternal salvation. The pattern of redemption shown clearly. Justification by faith was offered and given in the waning moments of the second criminal's life. An eternity of hope was broadcast in Jesus' words to him. Even before Christ died, the exchange of words between Him and the two criminals gives us the patterns for both eternal death and life. The repentant criminal's suffering on his cross could not dim the power of God's ultimate love. It was revealed as Jesus assured the man that he would be with Him that very day in paradise.

Christ was not surprised that these two criminals were to be His companions at Calvary. It was the fulfillment of the Scripture Jesus had quoted shortly before He was arrested. He prophesied to His disciples the words of Isaiah, and now, these Scriptures would be fulfilled. With Isaiah's words, Jesus revealed He would be *"numbered"* with the two criminals on that hill of death.

Luke 22:37 (NKJV)

"For I say to you that this which is written must still be accomplished in Me: 'And He was numbered with the transgressors.' For the things concerning Me have an end.'"

Isaiah 53:12 (NKJV)

"Therefore I will divide Him a portion with the great, And He shall divide the spoil with the strong, Because He poured out His soul unto death, And He was numbered with the transgressors, And He bore the sin of many, And made intercession for the transgressors."

Into the Father's Hands

Luke 23:44-45 (NKJV)

"Now it was about the sixth hour, and there was darkness over all the earth until the ninth hour. {45} Then the sun was darkened, and the veil of the temple was torn in two."

The hours, the minutes, and even the seconds must have passed with agonizing slowness. The torture seemed endless. Then, the sixth hour (noon) came. The sun would have been high in the sky. Yet, it ceased to shine. Darkness covered the earth like a thick blanket. As this was happening, the veil of the temple, the protective covering that kept all eyes from the Holy of Holies, was ripped completely in two. It was as if the hands of the Father, in all His majestic power, seized the barrier between Him and humankind and split it wide open. Imagine what it was like for those in the temple, gazing through the unexpected darkness and seeing this terrible, even terrifying sight. Religion, as they knew it, would no longer make coming to God the privilege of a single high priest. It was finished. Something other than Christ was dying. Something new had begun.

Luke 23:46 (NKJV)

" And when Jesus had cried out with a loud voice, He said, "Father, 'into Your hands I commit My spirit.'"" Having said this, He breathed His last."

Party Time in Hell? Not for Long

As Jesus breathed His last, a yoke of despair came to rest upon the backs of the disciples and all of His followers who were there. John took Mary, the mother of Jesus, under his wing. Without hope, they left Golgotha. Imagine the feelings of utter confusion, fear and loss in every one of them. At this moment, with death finally coming upon Jesus, all hell began to celebrate. The devilish party lasted until, on the third day, the Lion of Judah rose and took His rightful place.

The party in hell was over. Jesus was alive! As you read the verses below, imagine how the angel's announcement affected not only the three women at Christ's empty tomb, but also how your life and mine were forever changed.

Mark 16:1-6 (NKJV)

"Now when the Sabbath was past, Mary Magdalene, Mary the mother of James, and Salome bought spices, that they might come and anoint Him. {2} Very early in the morning, on the first day of the week, they came to the tomb when the sun had risen. {3} And they said among themselves, "Who will roll away the stone from the door of the tomb for us?" {4} But when they looked up, they saw that the stone had been rolled away; for it was very large. {5} And entering the tomb, they saw a young man clothed in a long white robe sitting on the right side; and they were alarmed. {6} But he said to them, "Do not be alarmed. You seek Jesus of Nazareth, who was crucified. He is risen! He is not here. See the place where they laid Him.""

"He is risen! He is not here."

In the next chapter, we will explore how the book was closed on the past. What seemed to be the end was only the beginning. Christ the King was alive. The Lamb's Book of Life opened its pages and names began to be written in it by the hand of the Most High. Fear, disappointment and confusion had lost their power. Jesus' instructions on prayer, in Matthew, Chapter 6, now made complete sense.

Matthew 6:9-10 (NKJV)

"In this manner, therefore, pray: Our Father in heaven, Hallowed be Your name. {10} Your kingdom come. Your will be done On earth as it is in heaven."

Five

The End was only the Beginning.

ঙ৪০ঙ৪০ 13 ঙ৪০ঙ৪০

His Victory Declared - *"He is not here"*

Luke 24:6a (NKJV)

"He is not here, but is risen!"[19]

The resurrected Christ now appeared to His disciples and spent many days with them. He ate with them, walked and talked with them and taught them many things. Then, He ascended to the Father. The story seemed complete. However, it was only the beginning. God's kingdom had come. The Father's will had been accomplished. The future of God's sons and daughters was now bright and unending.

To put what we have looked at into proper perspective, we must turn to Jesus' words to His disciples, as they were recorded in John, Chapter 16. The disciples had been given the explanation. However, they could not fully understand it until the resurrected Christ came to them. They needed the events of His death, burial and resurrection to occur before they could fill in the blanks and comprehend what Jesus had told them. What Jesus had said was now about to become clear. He was among them to fulfill the will of the Father. His ascension would signal the time when He would send the Holy Spirit. The Spirit would be another Comforter just like Christ. He would be our Comforter. John records this.

---

[19] Also, Mark 16:1-6

Let us begin with this one verse from John, Chapter 15 and then go to John, Chapter 16 as Jesus completes His explanation. Keep in mind that the disciples could not yet fully grasp what He was saying.

John 15:26 (NKJV)

"But when the Helper comes, whom I shall send to you from the Father, the Spirit of truth who proceeds from the Father, He will testify of Me."

John 16:5-15 (NKJV)

"But now I go away to Him who sent Me, and none of you asks Me, 'Where are You going?' {6} But because I have said these things to you, sorrow has filled your heart. {7} Nevertheless I tell you the truth. It is to your advantage that I go away; for if I do not go away, the Helper will not come to you; but if I depart, I will send Him to you. {8} And when He has come, He will convict the world of sin, and of righteousness, and of judgment: {9} of sin, because they do not believe in Me; {10} of righteousness, because I go to My Father and you see Me no more; {11} of judgment, because the ruler of this world is judged. {12} I still have many things to say to you, but you cannot bear them now. {13} However, when He, the Spirit of truth, has come, He will guide you into all truth; for He will not speak on His own authority, but whatever He hears He will speak; and He will tell you things to come. {14} He will glorify Me, for He will take of what is

Mine and declare it to you. {15} All things that the Father has are Mine. Therefore I said that He will take of Mine and declare it to you."

Our Great Advantage

John 16:7 (NKJV)

"Nevertheless I tell you the truth. It is to your advantage that I go away; for if I do not go away, the Helper will not come to you; but if I depart, I will send Him to you."

Jesus knew the plan of heaven would be incomplete until the Holy Spirit came to fill the void left by His (the Lord's) earthly departure. He also knew His disciples would be deeply saddened and confused until the course of events was finished. Only then, would they remember His words and understand. Jesus was sensitive to the sorrow the disciples would soon be feeling. What was to come would be a shock to them. Jesus could not prevent this. He could not stop their feelings from overwhelming them. What He could do, and did, was to leave them with words of hope that they would remember at His post-crucifixion appearances. Therefore, He spoke of the necessity of His leaving so He could send the Holy Spirit.

John 16:8-11 (NKJV)

"And when He has come, He will convict the world of sin, and of righteousness, and of judgment: {9} of sin, because they do not believe in Me; {10} of righteousness, because

*I go to My Father and you see Me no more;
{11} of judgment, because the ruler of this
world is judged."*

John 16:8-11 records the divine outline of the Holy Spirit's threefold purpose for coming here among us. Jesus said that the Spirit will *"convict"* the world of sin, righteousness and judgment. The term *"convict"* (*"elegcho,"* in the original Greek language used by John) means, *"to convict, convince, tell a fault, rebuke, reprove."*[20]

1. The Spirit will *"convict"* the world of sin.

2. The Spirit will *"convict"* the world of righteousness.

As He convicts the world of sin, the Holy Spirit offers hope in the form of an alternative, which is justification leading to righteousness. The repentant sinner has a freely given opportunity to replace all that offends the Father with His gift of righteousness. This is explained in one of the Paul's great doctrinal statements about justification and redemption, that he wrote to the Romans.

Romans 8:1-2 (NKJV)

"There is therefore now no condemnation to those who are in Christ Jesus, who do not walk according to the flesh, but according to the Spirit. {2} For the law of the Spirit of life in Christ Jesus has made me free from the law of sin and death."

3. The Spirit will convict the world of judgment. He will announce to all, that the world's righteous Judge, Jesus

---

[20] QuickVerse 4 © 1992-1997 by Craig Rairden and Parsons' Technology , Inc. All Rights Reserved. (Computer program)

Christ, now sits on the throne of divine authority and power. This serves as both a promise and a warning. Everyone will make personal choices that one day will determine each person's standing. This will come in that inevitable day when we all stand before the Father's holy throne and books are opened. The choice is clear for us today. It is either a righteous life in the Spirit or death in the carnal ways of sin.

John the Revelator (also the author of the Gospel and Epistles of John) provided us with this awesome, confirming report of what He saw in the Spirit, while in exile on the Isle of Patmos. As the lone surviving apostle, John was given the honor of writing the conclusion to the Bible. As we read it, we see how all of Christ's words and all of His deeds will lead to the fulfillment of every prophetic truth, recorded and verified through the sixty-six books of Scripture.

Revelation 20:11-12 (NKJV)

"Then I saw a great white throne and Him who sat on it, from whose face the earth and the heaven fled away. And there was found no place for them. {12} And I saw the dead, small and great, standing before God, and books were opened. And another book was opened, which is the Book of Life. And the dead were judged according to their works, by the things which were written in the books."

As I reflect on the inevitability of Revelation, Chapter 20, I cannot help but look back again to The Lord's Prayer. When the books will be opened, and the Book of Life is read, there will be no arguments, no negotiations and no opportunities to plead for mercy. Christ's substitutionary atonement will be the only basis for salvation. Choices that we previously freely made will determine the outcomes of our eternal destinies. God, help us all to accept Christ's invitation to *"take the water of life freely"* in your kingdom forever!

Matthew 6:13b (NKJV)

"For Yours is the kingdom and the power and the glory forever. Amen."

Revelation 22:17 (NKJV)

"And the Spirit and the bride say, "Come!" And let him who hears say, 'Come!" And let him who thirsts come. Whoever desires, let him take the water of life freely.""

Your Great Opportunity

As you read this, have you heard the Holy Spirit saying, *"Come"*? Have you given your heart to Jesus? Have you accepted forgiveness and redemption? If not, it is the easiest invitation to accept you will ever have. God sees your heart. All I can do is offer a helping prayer. You need only pray this or something like it. I pray that you do because you will be answering God's invitation to *"Come."*

Father, in Jesus name, let your name be holy in my life. I come to you just as I am. I surrender to your will. I repent of my sin and call Jesus my Savior. I believe He is the risen Son of God and accept Him as my Lord. I ask that you save me. Thank you for forgiving me and presenting me with the gift of eternal life. I am yours and will honor and love You forever. Amen.

ഌ഍ഄ഍ 14 ഄ഍ഄ഍

His Gift to Us
Unceasing Intercession

Jesus taught us to pray. He gave us an example to follow in His prayer life and He continues to pray on our behalf. Jesus' advocacy with the Father is a constant demonstration of His love. It shows itself in His ever-present, dependable and unceasing intercession to the Father for us. This is all possible because of His atoning, sacrificial death on the cross, His resurrection and ascendance to the throne.

Romans 8:34 (NKJV)

"Who is he who condemns? It is Christ who died, and furthermore is also risen, who is even at the right hand of God, who also makes intercession for us."

Hebrews 7:24-27 (NKJV)

"But He, because He continues forever, has an unchangeable priesthood. {25} Therefore He is also able to save to the uttermost those who come to God through Him, since He always lives to make intercession for them. {26} For such a High Priest was fitting for us, who is holy, harmless, undefiled, separate from

sinners, and has become higher than the heavens; {27} who does not need daily, as those high priests, to offer up sacrifices, first for His own sins and then for the people's, for this He did once for all when He offered up Himself."

You will find this heavenly system of intercession to be flawless and completely effective. Your understanding of Jesus' powerful gift of intercession will broaden, as you embrace this blanket of divine care that covers all the children of God. It paints a picture of the powerful invitation contained in Jesus' instructions within The Lord's Prayer. In Matthew 6:5, Jesus begins with the words *"When you pray..."* A second report of this same discourse is found in Luke 11:1-2. Verse 1 shows the disciples asking Jesus to teach them to pray. Verse 2 is His response.

Luke 11:1-2 (NKJV)

"Now it came to pass, as He was praying in a certain place, when He ceased, that one of His disciples said to Him, "Lord, teach us to pray, as John also taught his disciples." {2} So He said to them, "When you pray, say: Our Father in heaven, Hallowed be Your name. Your kingdom come. Your will be done On earth as it is in heaven."

Luke makes it apparent that Christ's unceasing intercession ties together God's will with the coming of His kingdom. The loving gift of intercession has been delivered to us so we can pray with assurance to our heavenly, *"hallowed"* Father. Once again, we find a parallel to Verses 9-10 of Matthew 6. As we have seen in earlier chapters, prayer begins as an expression of human petition with reverence and deference to our heavenly Father. The Father answers. His kingdom comes and His will is done.

Hebrews 7:26 reveals another truth, regarding this loving gift of intercession that we have been given.

Hebrews 7:26 (NKJV)

"For such a High Priest was fitting for us, who is holy, harmless, undefiled, separate from sinners, and has become higher than the heavens;"

The writer to the Hebrews tells us that Jesus, in His sinless perfection, *"has become higher than the heavens."* Because He is our perfect Intercessor, who lives forever and inhabits the highest throne of authority, we are guaranteed favor as petitioners to the Father. This favor is not to be taken lightly. Favor is our gift, and fully a demonstration of godly grace. As with His intercession itself, the favor of God has its foundations in His love. When Jesus prayed to the Father on our behalf in John, Chapter 17, He made it clear that the Father's favor for us has His divine love as its foundation.

John 17:23 (NKJV)

"I in them, and You in Me; that they may be made perfect in one, and that the world may know that You have sent Me, and have loved them as You have loved Me."

The Godhead has extended to us, through the perfect plan of divine love, the opportunity to embrace this circle of heavenly unity and become a part of it. We can look at this as simply a spiritual oneness. However, to understand it fully, we need to see the plan's entire nature. Jesus said, *"I in them..."* His words frame a picture of an inseparable bonding and intertwining. This intertwining or interlocking occurs when our salvation brings the risen Christ to live *"in"* us. The scriptural extension of this takes us to the Holy Spirit. He too, is in us in the same way. Now we see intercessory prayer as a complex, interlocking weave of Father, Son, Spirit... and us.

ःॐ৪ঙॐ 15 ःॐ৪ঙॐ

Our Gift to Him - Loving, Committed and Fruitful Service

I cannot help but reflect on all the years that the Father has granted me to walk in His grace-filled favor. He has provided my daily bread in good times and bad. He has forgiven my trespasses. They have surely been great. His forgiveness has always been greater. He has kept me from temptation. He has stood firmly and faithfully between the evil one and me. Finally, He has allowed me to experience the joy of worshiping and fellowshipping with Him.

I often have wondered what I could give back to Him that would really please Him. He does not seem to demand much. In His loving grace, He permits me to get away with far more than I would have allowed my children when they were growing up. The Word is clear about one thing. Faith is required to please Him. Hebrews 11:6 (NKJV) tells us that *"...without faith it is impossible to please Him..."* Scripture also tells us that beyond having faith, we ought to make it our aim to be *"well pleasing to Him."* I believe this covers everything and answers every question about living life.

2 Corinthians 5:9 (NKJV)

"Therefore we make it our aim, whether present or absent, to be well pleasing to Him."

Hebrews 13:20-21 (NKJV)

"Now may the God of peace who brought up our Lord Jesus from the dead, that great Shepherd of the sheep, through the blood of the everlasting covenant, {21} make you complete in every good work to do His will, working in you what is well pleasing in His sight, through Jesus Christ, to whom be glory forever and ever. Amen."

Here is part of my personal list of things I can do that will be *"well pleasing to Him."* They make great guidelines for my life (and perhaps, yours). They are the foundations of a sure testimony of who the Father is, as they reflect His character in me.

1. I ought to do everything I can to honor His desires for me to be *"well pleasing to Him."* I can do this by living an honest, transparently grateful life.

2. I ought to be a positive, godly influence on the world He loves so dearly. My attitudes, actions and especially, my reactions to others should make a consistent difference.

3. I ought to strive to be a reflection of His holiness and purity. Though I am far from perfect, my daily life can shine brightly as a testimony to His faithfulness.

What are your basic guidelines for pleasing the Lord? You can start by establishing a few, for a life that is pleasing to God. As you seek the Lord, you can add others to your list. If you will do this, you will increase your impact on the world around you. In the process, you will become just a little bit more like Jesus every day and in every way. The

Father, day after day, will be well pleased that you are doing so… and I know you will also be pleased.

On that same day in which Jesus gave us The Lord's Prayer, He described us as, *"the light of the world"* and *"a city that is set on a hill that cannot be hidden."* He was speaking of our potential. He was voicing the desire of the Father.

Matthew 5:14-16 (NKJV)

> *"You are the light of the world. A city that is set on a hill cannot be hidden. {15} Nor do they light a lamp and put it under a basket, but on a lampstand, and it gives light to all who are in the house. {16} Let your light so shine before men, that they may see your good works and glorify your Father in heaven."*

I am sure I could write a number of chapters on Matthew 5:14-16. However, that will be for another book at another time. As we conclude "Focused on the Father - The Lord's Prayers," I pray that you, and all those who will read these pages, will let your light shine brightly, always and in all ways, glorifying your Father in heaven.

With every blessing, *Dr. Bob Abramson*

- - - - - - - - - - - - - - - - -

On the final page of the book, look once more at my complete amplified paraphrase of The Lord's Prayer. Then, live it as consistently as you can.

151

My Complete Amplified Paraphrase

Our incredible and perfect Father of Mercy and Grace, Who rules and reigns in majesty in the place of complete and undeniable authority, let your name be revered and worshiped, as we behold the beauty of your holiness.

{10} Father, let all that makes up your wisdom and accomplishes your divine purposes be fully done in this place, in this hour, just as it has always been done in heaven, which is the seat of your merciful, just and sovereign supremacy.

{11} Father, Provide us with those things that will sustain our natural and physical needs through the day and give us your presence in our lives today!

{12} And cancel the enormous debt we owe you, just as we willingly cancel and forgive every wrong and every debt owed to us by anyone.

{13a} Be the One who faithfully intervenes when temptation tries to intrude on our lives.{13b} And bring us through the trials and temptations that would test our faithfulness to You and deliver us from the evil one himself ...along with deliverance from the essential character of every evil thing that opposes you, Father. {13c} We acknowledge that Your incredible majesty, never-ending splendor and divine brilliance are a shining light, without end. What we have prayed is truthful and we agree with it. We affirm with our voices and believe in our hearts that it shall come to pass.

About Dr. Bob Abramson

Dr. Abramson has extensive experience as a cross-cultural mentor and trainer of those in the five-fold ministry. He and his wife Nancy have pastored international churches in New York City and the Fiji Islands in the South Pacific. He established or taught in Bible schools and ministry training centers in New Zealand, Fiji, Taiwan, Hong Kong, Malaysia, Europe and the United States. He provides free resources worldwide through his website, "Mentoring Ministry" (www.mentoringministry.com).

Dr. Abramson earned a Doctor of Ministry from Erskine Theological Seminary, a Masters in Religion from Liberty University and a Bachelor of Arts in the Bible with a minor in Systematic Theology from Southeastern University. He and his wife Nancy live in Lake Worth, Florida. They have five grown children and six grandchildren.

Contact Dr. Abramson, at www.mentoringministry.com
or write him at Dr.Bob@mentoringministry.com

Dr. Abramson is also the author of these books.
- "Just a Little Bit More - The Heart of a Mentor" (Book and Workbook)
- "The Leadership Puzzle"
  (Two Workbooks and Facilitator's Manual)
- "Growing Together, Marriage Enrichment for Every Culture." (Book and Workbook)
- "Reflections, Volumes One and Two," the first two in a continuing series of devotional journals
- "Moral Manhood - Swimming with the Sharks"

www.ingramcontent.com/pod-product-compliance
Lightning Source LLC
LaVergne TN
LVHW021453080426
835509LV00018B/2269